MW01089282

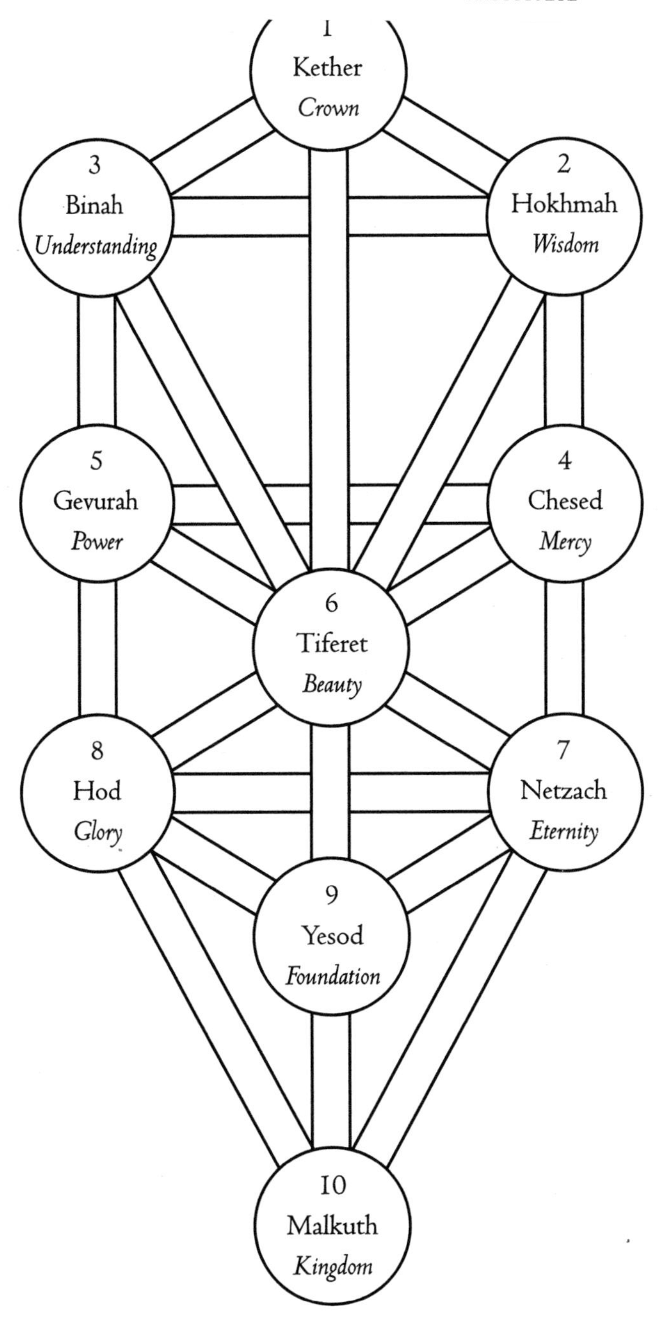
1
Kether
Crown
2
Hokhmah
Wisdom
3
Binah
Understanding
4
Chesed
Mercy
5
Gevurah
Power
6
Tiferet
Beauty
7
Netzach
Eternity
8
Hod
Glory
9
Yesod
Foundation
10
Malkuth
Kingdom

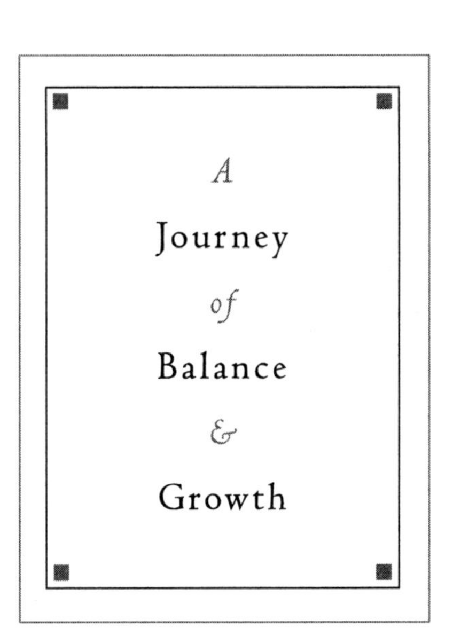
A
Journey
of
Balance
&
Growth

About the Author

Rachel Pollack is a poet, an award-winning novelist, a world authority on the modern interpretation of Tarot cards, and a Tarot card artist. Her novel *Godmother Night* won the 1997 World Fantasy Award. Her earlier novel, *Unquenchable Fire*, won the Arthur C. Clarke Award.

She has published twelve books on the Tarot, including *Seventy-Eight Degrees of Wisdom*, often called "the Bible of Tarot readers," and is the creator of the Shining Tribe Tarot. Her books have been published in nine languages. Rachel lives in New York's Hudson Valley.

About the Artist

Hermann Haindl was born in 1927 in Berlin, Germany. In 1944, at the age of seventeen, he was summoned to the Nazi German army and a few weeks later he was a prisoner of war. He spent three and a half years in a prisoners' camp in Kiev, Ukraine. Here he had several near-death experiences, through being shot and contracting disease.

When he came back to Germany he was 90 percent handicapped from the war and captivity in prison camp. His mother was a refugee in West Germany. After this long time outside of normal society, it was difficult to come back to everyday life and find a job. At last he started a new career at the theater in Frankfurt am Main as a stage designer and as director of the theater's art workshops. He was one of the most famous theater painters in Germany, and worked for theaters in Bayreuth and Barcelona together with the best-known stage designers in the 60s and 70s. In 1973, Golda Meir asked him to paint a huge picture of nearly 300 meters of history and landscapes for the twenty-fifth anniversary of the founding of the state of Israel. He taught master classes at the universities of Jerusalem and Bayreuth and at the theater-school in Recklinghausen, Germany.

When he was fifty years old, he left the theater and started a new career as a free painter. In his experience of the vast risk of life, he sought to integrate spirituality and art. Through worldwide travel he found an approach to the cultures of indigenous people and sought ancient philosophic wisdom in Europe. In this way he found the Tarot and also the Kabbalah. In accordance with the rules of the historic brotherhood of the Golden Dawn he painted his own Tarot cards, and later the Kabbalah tree to be used together with the Tarot cards.

In 1985, when the Droemer-Knaur publishing house came to know about his Tarot cards, they put Hermann Haindl in contact with Rachel Pollack. This became the basis of a life-long cooperation and friendship between them.

Includes Haindl's *Tree of Life* Poster

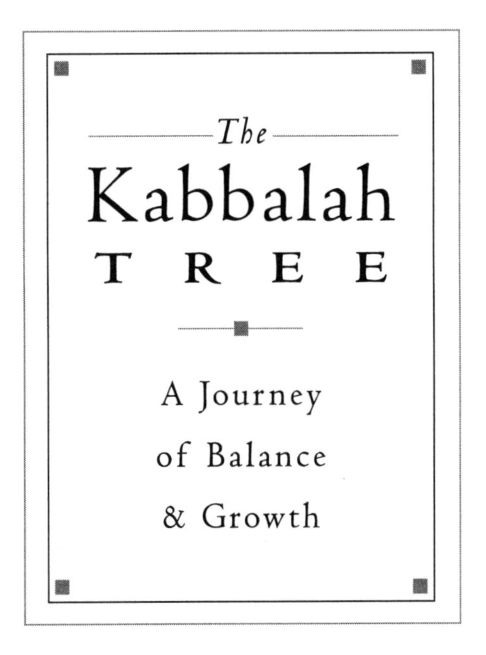

The Kabbalah TREE

A Journey of Balance & Growth

RACHEL POLLACK

2004
Llewellyn Publications
St. Paul, Minnesota 55164-0383, U.S.A.

FIRST EDITION
First Printing, 2004

Book design and editing by Rebecca Zins
Cover design by Kevin R. Brown
Cover and poster "Tree of Life" painting © Hermann Haindl
Interior illustrations by the Llewellyn Art Department

Library of Congress Cataloging-in-Publication Data
Pollack, Rachel
The kabbalah tree: a journey of balance & growth / Rachel Pollack; includes Haindl's Tree of Life poster. —1st ed.
p. cm.
Includes bibliographical references (p.).
ISBN 0-7387-0507-1
1. Tree of Life. I. Title.
BL444.P65 2004
135'.47—dc22

2004044134

Llewellyn Publications
A Division of Llewellyn Worldwide, Ltd.
P.O. Box 64383, Dept. 0-7387-0507-1
St. Paul, MN 55164-0383, U.S.A.
www.llewellyn.com

Printed in the United States of America
on recycled paper

Contents

Dedication

To Avigayil Landsman, Reb Avigayil the Sage, extraordinary teacher and devoted friend. May the One who blessed all our ancestors bless her with health and continued brilliance. *Keyn y'hi ra'tzon.*

Preface
Hermann Haindl and Me

The first I ever heard of Hermann Haindl was a phone call from Gerhard Riemann, at that time the editor of the company that published my first Tarot books in German. "We're about to publish a new Tarot deck by a German artist," Gerhard said to me, "would you be interested to write the text?" I assumed he meant the LWB (little white booklet) that comes with virtually every Tarot deck, and told him that that would be fine. A few days later, Hermann and his wife Erica came to my apartment in Amsterdam, their arms full of astonishing paintings.

I had never seen Tarot pictures like these before, not just for their artistic mastery but for their range and depth of spiritual experience. As I would get to know Hermann, I would learn of his young years as a German prisoner of war in a brutal Russian camp, of his horror after the war when he discovered what his nation had done. I would learn as well that instead of despair Hermann turned to a lifelong search for beauty and the divine and moral responsibility. His paintings reflected journeys to sacred centers in India, initiation rituals in Native America, and ancient temples in Egypt.

At that first meeting, however, I knew only that this small project would clearly take more time and effort than I had imagined. So after that initial look I asked the cards if I should do this project. They were very enthusiastic, with images of cooperation, understanding, and success. Instead of a little white booklet I ended up writing five hundred pages on the Haindl Tarot, published in English in two volumes.

That was in the mid-1980s. A decade or more later, I had a similar experience when Hermann and Erica called me from Germany to say that Hermann had painted a large canvas of the Tree of Life from the

Kabbalah, and he would like me to write a book to go with it. This time I knew better than to expect some small task.

But the task was huge in different ways than my work on the Haindl Tarot. Though I found Hermann's Tarot pictures a challenge I considered, rightly or wrongly, that I had a good grounding in the Tarot itself. This new project was different. I had studied and worked with Kabbalah and the Tree of Life, yet I knew very well that there were people, some of them even my friends, who knew much more about the subject than I had. They had devoted their lives to its study, just as brilliant people have done for thousands of years. I told Hermann that other people knew the tree and its history better than I did, but he said that other people did not know his art like I did.

Some days later a poster-sized photograph arrived of the remarkable painting featured in this book. I realized that Hermann had brought to life what too often becomes an abstract diagram. And I realized as well that this would be one of the themes that I would try to evoke.

To write this book I immersed myself in the tradition of the tree, other aspects of Kabbalah, interpretations of Genesis (where the Tree of Life image originates), and the worldwide myth of a tree that grows from earth to heaven. Once again, my association with Hermann Haindl has opened me to knowledge and understanding.

Acknowledgments

A work on Kabbalah is a massive undertaking, only begun with the understanding that there are many who have immersed themselves in these waters all their lives, and who know how to dive deeper, and swim further, than I could even attempt. I have drawn on many sources in my attempt to say something of these wonders, and if I have misrepresented anyone's ideas or beliefs I ask their forgiveness, and the forgiveness of any readers I may unknowingly lead astray.

A special thank-you to Judith Laura, for bringing together—and stating so clearly—wide areas of knowledge and insight. For support, and ideas and knowledge, I want to thank the members of exoteric-l, a community of loving and brilliant people. I thank Rabbi Lamed ben Clifford for his wide-ranging knowledge and recognition that a garden is a place to play. As my teacher, Ioanna Salajan, said many years ago, "Nothing is learned except through joy." To Zoe Matoff, whose spirit and mind shine so brightly, I owe more than I can say.

Finally, my deep gratitude, once again, to Hermann and Erica Haindl, for all their generosity and brilliance.

She is a Tree of Life for those who cling to her.

HEBREW PRAYER
sung on returning the Torah to the ark

And I beheld the Tree of Life,

The Tree of Destiny,

The way of all things, and

Its folded bark was iron, and rust

lay new in every crease.

The morning dew giving life and death.

And upon its crown

lay thick the leaves and leaves,

and leaves uncounted

each with their own writing

and each in His own Book.

HERCEL V. SHULTZ
Houses in the Tree of Life

Introduction

Our world exists in time, in a history that does not just stretch into the past but unfolds constantly, with ever more surprises. A century ago, you could hardly find a subject more abstruse or forgotten than the esoteric tradition known as Kabbalah. Only a tiny handful of people had ever heard of it, let alone studied it or tried to bring its wisdom into their own lives. To many of those who did know of it, it seemed overly complicated and medieval, hardly suitable for the new, modern, twentieth century.

Kabbalah is a Jewish mystical tradition, with ideas first developed two thousand years ago, and most elaborated from the twelfth century onwards. The Hebrew word *Kabbalah* means "received," as an oral teaching is received by a student directly from a teacher, or perhaps in revelation, directly from God. And yet it was not primarily Jews who kept the tradition alive a hundred years ago, it was a small group of occultists, Christians with great interest in Pagan as well as Jewish traditions. Their main influence outside secret initiatory groups seemed to be among artists and writers seeking an underpinning of meaning to their creative impulses. Growing up in an Orthodox Jewish home in the 1950s I did not even hear the word *Kabbalah* until, as an adult, I discovered Tarot cards and began to learn their spiritual and interpretive tradition.

And now, as we begin the twenty-first century, this mysterious, ancient teaching has sprung up everywhere. Movie stars go on talk shows to proudly proclaim that Kabbalah has changed their lives. Books appear telling us how to use Kabbalah to have good marriages and successful careers. Kabbalah's most famous symbol, a diagram known as the Tree of Life (in Hebrew *aytz chayim*) now shows up on greeting cards and silver necklaces. Such are the wonders of history.

This book concerns that symbol, that marvelous tree. In particular, it explores a special version of that symbol, a lush painting by Hermann Haindl, a man who has dedicated his life to art as a spiritual path. Haindl is probably best known for the Tarot cards he painted some twenty years ago. Brilliant and complex and filled with meaning, they became one of the most popular Tarots of recent decades.

Even then, Haindl was interested in Kabbalah, for he painted a Hebrew letter on each card, a tradition that goes back to those occultists more than a hundred years ago (see chapter two, on the history of the tree). Now he has given new life to the tree image, with some of the same themes he developed in the cards—the sacredness of the earth; the power of very old images; the holy wisdom of indigenous peoples, especially from Native America; the way nothing in nature ever stays the same but over time transforms, one thing into another, animals and trees into stone, stone into life.

The tree symbol comes from a tradition that bases itself on ecstatic awareness of the divine. At its heart its power is not intellectual but revelatory. And yet so many teachers have pondered it, and written about it in such complex ways, we can all too easily let it become a purely abstract study of ideas, with long lists of attributes the student tries to memorize. The tree itself can appear a sort of geometric diagram rather than a living image. What Hermann Haindl has done is make this ancient symbol fully a Tree of *Life*. His painting teems with life, like some magnificent rain forest of the mind. We see birds, and snakes, and animals, and faces. We can make out ancient mythological beings, and Jesus, and faces made of eroded stone. His tree is no less mystical for giving us such richness of life. Instead, he reminds us that all knowledge of the divine begins in nature—nature and the human mind as it looks with wonder at the glory of existence.

In its common form, the tree symbol looks like this.

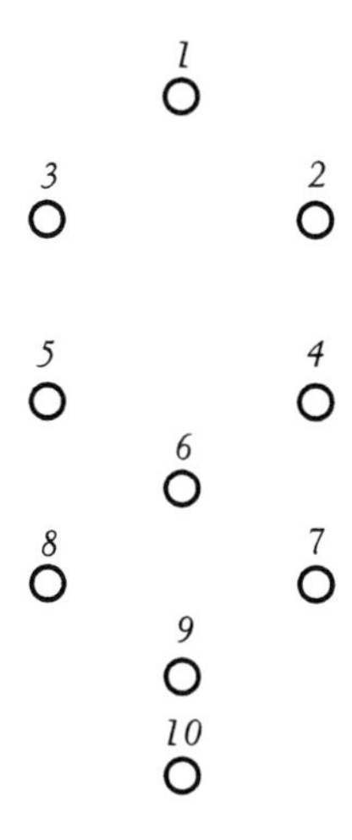

These ten circles represent ten pulses, or emanations, of divine energy, called in Hebrew *sephiroth* (sephiroth is the plural form of *sephirah*), a word derived from *sappir*, the Hebrew for "sapphire." Kabbalah teaches us that God did not create the world in one stroke but in stages, with the sephiroth as the means and the pattern for existence. You can see the Hebrew names for the sephiroth, with their usual translations, on the painting, but here is a list, from the top down:

1. Kether—Crown
2. Hokhmah—Wisdom
3. Binah—Understanding
4. Chesed—Mercy
5. Gevurah—Power
6. Tiferet—Beauty
7. Netzach—Eternity
8. Hod—Glory
9. Yesod—Foundation
10. Malkuth—Kingdom

Some readers may know slightly different spellings for some of the sephiroth; for example, Chokmah instead of Hokhmah. Do not let this worry you. The Hebrew alphabet is different than the Latin, and there simply is no precise rule for how to transliterate words. The very word "Kabbalah" has many variants, such as "Qabalah" and "Cabala." Some of these have actually become associated with different branches of the tradition. For example, Cabala is favored by Christians who have adapted the tree and its symbols to Christian concepts (for example, placing Christ in the center, at Tiferet). Qabalah, on the other hand, often refers to the non-Jewish occult tradition called Western, or Hermetic. For the sake of simplicity, I will use Kabbalah as the standard spelling throughout, and try to make clear when I am referring to the Jewish, Christian, or Western Hermetic concepts and symbolism.

According to all these traditions, the divine Creator sent the energy down in a specific pattern from Kether to Malkuth. At the same time, that pattern is not the only way we can connect the sephiroth. Because the Hebrew language has twenty-two letters, Kabbalists long ago developed the idea of twenty-two connecting lines, or pathways, between the ten sephiroth. Below we see, on the left, the pattern of Creation, and on the right, the most common version of the twenty-two pathways. This version actually belongs to the Western tradition more than the Jewish, but it's the one most people know and, in fact, it's the one Hermann Haindl used as the basis for his painting.

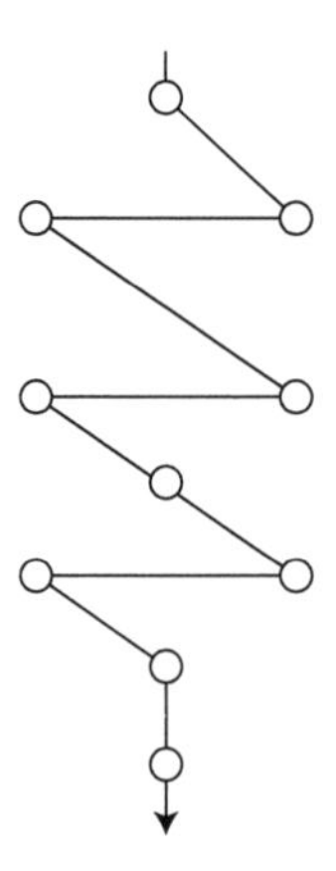

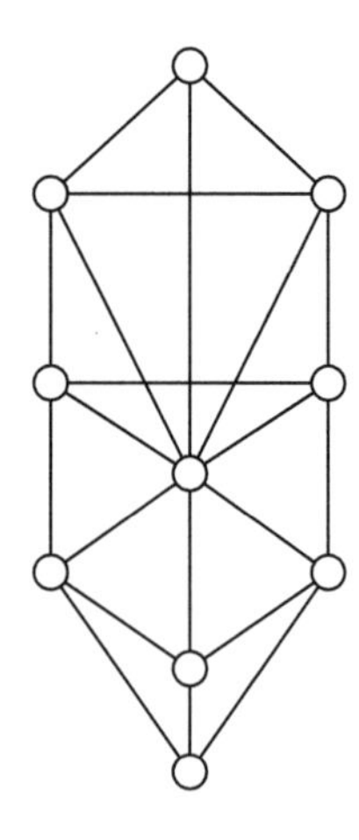

Because there are so many variations on Kabbalah—within the Jewish tradition alone the rabbis often went in different directions—we can sometimes get lost in the contradictions or, worse, take one version as absolute truth and ignore any other approaches. I have tried here to draw from all these approaches wherever useful (and within the limits of my knowledge), and at the same time attempt to put them together in a story readers can follow, hopefully without too much confusion. Hermann Haindl's painting will help ground us by giving us a visual anchor.

The Kabbalah tree has its roots in Jewish mysticism, and inevitably we will explore the points of view of the rabbis who developed it. This does not mean that you need to be Jewish to appreciate it. As the traditions of Western and Christian Kabbalah clearly demonstrate, the tree operates very well as a symbol for many systems of belief. It really has grown into a kind of organizing principle for our human efforts to understand the world.

Because the tree is not just a narrow religious concept, we will draw on some unusual sources in our attempt to understand its message. This will include tribal and shamanic traditions, and also modern science. As well as the great rabbis we will look to contemporary Kabbalists, Tarot interpreters, and even a comic book writer who has explored the tree vividly and in great depth in his stories.

We will encounter the word "God" very often in these pages, as well as words and passages from the Bible. The tree is, after all, a Western symbol, and Western traditions are rooted in the Bible. At the same time, none of this is meant to support narrow religious ideas. Kabbalah is a mysterious journey of transformation, and one of the things it transforms is what we mean when we say "God." I ask, therefore, that readers set aside their previous beliefs, and especially any negative experiences they may have had in their own religious upbringing. Sadly, there are far too many of these.

The symbol is a living tree. It continues to change, and adapt, and accept new ideas. While it comes from a background that is patriarchal, we do not need to accept the strict separation of male and female qualities, or the implied superiority of the masculine that sometimes seems to pervade earlier centuries of mystical thought. Instead, we can allow our own contemporary wisdom to add to the great store of teachings over the centuries.

This does not mean we reject the dedication or brilliance of earlier times. It would be worse than arrogant, it would be simple ignorance to dismiss the great achievements of such figures as the sixteenth-century Rabbi Isaac Luria, or the mysterious author of the Book of Formation two thousand years ago, or the vast synthesis created by the Hermetic Order of the Golden Dawn in the late nineteenth century. But neither do we have to sweep away our own insights in a blind worship of the past.

In his Tarot deck, and now in his painting of the tree, Hermann Haindl imbues these great traditions with his devotion to the earth and his reverence for archaic goddesses and all the world's traditions. This gives his version of the Tree of Life a slightly different character from the familiar abstract diagram. It does not change the meaning of the tree, but adds to it, helping to reinvigorate this centuries-old symbol for a new century.

ONE

The Tree *and the* Ladder

Think of the image of a tree. Strong, graceful, its branches reach up like long fingers into the sky. It is hundreds, maybe thousands of years old. And now think of a tree older than all, a tree whose trunk and branches connect heaven and earth, whose roots reach down into the dark mysteries below our normal consciousness, into the very origins of existence; a tree of dreams, a tree of beauty, a tree of God. A tree of life. Is our world, with all its complications, hopes, and dangers, no more than a child's treehouse set in a vast tree that stretches through worlds upon worlds?

Now play with this image. If the tree is the connection of all life, does it begin in the dark underworld, stretch up through the existence we narrowly think of as "reality," and reach beyond to the spiritual heaven we imagine as somewhere far above our heads? But suppose all life, all existence begins with the Creator. Shouldn't the tree begin in "heaven"? And suppose our true home lies not in the world of pain and sorrow but in the divine perfection, what the legendary Welsh shaman/bard Taliesin called "the region of the summer stars." If the tree has its roots in heaven, and its branches reach *down* to us, does that mean that the tree grows upside down? Maybe *we* are upside down—that is, confused and seeing reality the wrong way around. If we could learn to see the true way, from the point of view of the divine rather than our ordinary "common sense" view (for that which is commonly agreed on is not necessarily true), then maybe the Tree of Life would stand revealed to us. And maybe we could learn to climb the tree and return to our roots as divine creations, made in the image of the Creator but ignorant of what that really means.

People climb trees. They find their way, branch by branch, into the higher regions. Before the invention of machines of flight—balloons, gliders, airplanes—giant trees were the only way people could leave the surface of the earth. So a tree becomes a ladder, and if the tree reaches high enough it becomes a ladder to heaven itself.

Now this is a literal image, and we should not confuse ourselves and believe there actually *is* a tree somewhere, or a giant ladder, that climbs up into the sky (why, in fact, should heaven be literally above us, in the sky?). And we should not believe that people in ancient times were much more simple-minded than our sophisticated selves, and so believed in such concrete trees and ladders. Images are metaphors, ways to make real in our minds what we understand as intuition.

A tree that reaches into heaven, however, is a very vivid and enticing metaphor, and so has proved useful to humans the world over as a way to formulate our desire to encounter the divine. In the set of traditions known as shamanism (the word comes from a specific people in Siberia but describes practices and religious approaches found wherever humans have lived), healers and visionaries travel in trance to the spirit world. To aid their journeys they use the literal image, sometimes a pole or even a small tree, sometimes a ladder. They will set this up in the ceremony, and when they enter trance they will experience a climb up the tree or ladder into the realm of the gods, where they may find some power object or even battle the spirits for the captured soul of a sick person.

Thirty years or so of books on shamanism and trance workshops have made such visions and journeys sound almost ordinary to modern people. At the same time, those of us who grew up in mainstream Western religious traditions may assume that our own culture contains no such trance climbs up a tree or a ladder. In fact, the Bible contains several such images. Most obviously, there is the Tree of Life itself, from the Garden of Eden, and we will look closely at just what this story tells us in a moment. But there also exists an image of a ladder that reaches from heaven to earth.

In the book of Genesis, Jacob has fled his brother's anger and is traveling in the wilderness. At night, in a place called Luz, he sets some stones for a pillow and goes to sleep. Now, stones set into a pile are themselves an image of the heavenly ascent, which is one reason why we find sacred pyramids in Egypt, Babylon, and Mexico, and why people in the Stone Age created mounds and giant hills so large they seem part of the natural landscape. Asleep, Jacob has "a vision in a dream." He sees a ladder set on the ground, reaching up all the way to heaven. Angels—the original Hebrew word means "messengers," for angels are messengers of the divine—ascend and descend. The power of the world above—the "kingdom of God," as a much later prophet, Jesus of Nazareth, son of Mary, called it—moves freely between the exalted existence of the divine and the difficult world of mortals.

Notice that the angels do not just descend from their realm to ours. Instead, they move in both directions, for if you have a ladder it does not go in only one direction. This, in fact, is a basic principle of esoteric ideas in general, and the Tree of Life in particular, that existence goes in both directions, from spirit "down" into physical matter, and from matter "up" into spirit. Neither is actually superior, for a full existence depends on both of them and the interchange between them. To really understand who we are we need to recognize that we, too, contain both spirit and matter, and that these qualities actually move up and down each other. When Watson, Crick, Wilkins, and Franklin discovered the double-spiral structure of DNA, the genetic basis of life, occultists recognized this as the same image found in spiritual teachings.

We might understand this double-spiral movement a little better if we think of the creative process in humans. And here we have an excellent example in Hermann Haindl himself. Haindl is the epitome of what we could call an intuitive artist. He will often begin a work by letting paint splash on the canvas and seeing what pictures seem to emerge. We should not make the mistake, however, of thinking he acts without thought. From this instinctive response he moves to a highly conceptual work in which his life experiences, political beliefs, and sacred knowledge all combine to form a coherent whole. We might say, therefore, that an original image "descends" down the tree or ladder into physical reality on the canvas. The act of painting, and the thought that goes into it, then "ascends" into a work of art that is as intellectual as it is visual.

In the Genesis story, Jacob does not himself travel up the ladder. Unlike the shamans, he does not ascend. In a sense, there is really no need, for in the next moment, God actually appears and speaks to Jacob directly, saying that Jacob's sons will become a great nation. When Jacob wakes up he names the place *Beth-el*, the "house of God," and calls it the "gate" of heaven for, he says, "God was in this place and I did not know it." These ideas, especially the gate, are also part of the shamanic, and later Kabbalist, idea of the tree, or ladder, that reaches to the realm of the divine. The Tree of Life is the path by which we climb to the sacred and then return to our true selves. Wherever and whenever we perceive it we find the gate of heaven. Jacob then marks the spot with yet another prehistoric image of the link between heaven and earth, a stone pillar.

The shamans often climb the ladder or tree to struggle, even battle, the gods for the sake of helpless humans. Jacob only watches. But maybe he simply is not yet ready. Kabbalist tradition suggests that a man must not begin the study of Kabbalah until he has married and fathered children—in other words, until he has become mature and responsible. Only then can he face the powerful forces hidden within the study and practices of Kabbalah. (These traditions originated in a patriarchal culture that only rarely recognized the possibility for women to enter into them. As with so much else, the introduction of women's points of view has radically opened new ideas and approaches to the Tree of Life and other aspects of Kabbalah.) Jacob, too, must become the master of his own life before he can go further in his knowledge of the divine.

Years after his dream vision, after he has married and begun his family, Jacob must once again confront his twin brother, with whom he has wrestled all his life, from their first moments in their mother's womb. Once more he sleeps in the wilderness, far from human civilization, with all its safety nets of assumed reality. This, too, is a shamanic experience, to find the sacred outside everyday life. Now, instead of a vision of powers that travel up and down a ladder, Jacob encounters a single figure, a "stranger" whose face he cannot quite see. And all night the two wrestle, neither one able to defeat the other.

Tradition identifies this figure as an angel but that is not what the text actually says. When Jacob demands a blessing from the mysterious figure, the stranger gives him a new name (another common shamanic experience), *Isra-el*, "one who has wrestled with God." Jacob then names the place *Peni-el*, the "face of God," for he says, "I have seen God face to face and survived." And having done this, Jacob finds the courage to go to his brother and seek peace.

As shamanic as this story is, it also is deeply Kabbalist. Though the ultimate truth of God lies beyond even the Tree of Life, the teachers identified aspects of the tree as a "greater" and "lesser face," and one goal of the study and meditation on the ten sephiroth becomes the ability to see those divine faces—and, like Jacob, survive the experience and then go on to seek peace. Jewish Kabbalists actually identify the "lesser face" as the central sephirah, Tiferet, which they also identify with Jacob, as the image of the perfect man; Christian Kabbalists see this sephirah as Christ.

With his two visions, the ladder and the struggle, Jacob embodies the very qualities of those shamans who use poles, ladders, pillars, and living trees as vehicles to ascend to the heavenly world and claim humanity's place among the divine. For this reason, another name for the Tree of Life, with its ten lights and twenty-two pathways, is Jacob's ladder.

The Tree of Life diagram developed over many centuries, beginning in the Middle Ages and the Renaissance and continuing to the late nineteenth century. Its origins—the roots of the tree, we might say—go back to the beginning of the Common Era (the term non-Christians use for the last two thousand years to avoid *anno domini*, "year of our lord"), with a remarkable work called the Sefer Yetsirah, the Book of Formation. In this very short text the anonymous writer first describes the sephiroth, the ten emanations of divine light, and the mystical power of the twenty-two Hebrew letters. The actual tree will be many centuries off, but this is where it began.

We will look at the Sefer Yetsirah more closely, but it is worth considering a religious mystical movement going on at that time in ancient Judaea for what it tells us about the origins of Kabbalah and its goals, and therefore for ways we can approach the Tree of Life, both in its diagram form and in Hermann Haindl's remarkable painting. Two thousand years ago, right around the time of the teachings of Jesus, Judaism faced a great crisis. Rome was trying to crush the Jewish desire to follow its own traditions, and in the year 70, in response to Jewish rebellion, the Roman army destroyed the vast Temple of Solomon that had stood as the center of Jewish ritual and spiritual life for hundreds of years.

Without the temple, and its seasonal rituals and sacrifices, how would people join themselves to God? The Sefer Yetsirah was, in fact, one answer, and it began a strain in mystical religion called "the work of creation," that is, the contemplation of the origins and structure of existence. Through meditation on the wonders of the sephiroth and the letters, and their place in the creation of the world, the mystic comes to a sense of the divine power that fills all existence, especially our own lives.

Another response was a kind of shamanic revival called "the work of the merkavah," or the work of the chariot. The chariot refers to a mystic vision described in the book of Ezekiel. Ezekiel lived during the Babylonian Exile, after the destruction of the first temple (Rome actually destroyed a second temple, rebuilt after the return from Babylon). His experience was therefore meaningful to those going through the pain of Roman attacks. The prophet described a highly detailed vision he had of a heavenly chariot, wheels within wheels and winged creatures with four faces. The merkavah mystics used this vision as their own vehicle for trance journeys into the seven *hekhaloth* (palaces) of heaven. The purpose of these journeys was to see the divine face to face, the very experience Jacob describes after his night of wrestling.

The great detail of the merkavah writings show that the journeyers considered the hekhaloth real places and not just hallucinations or subjective images. They warn of improper responses one might make at certain points in the journey. At the same time they recognized that all this took place on an inner level, stimulated by meditation and magical practices, for they described the experience as a "descent" to the chariot, even as the traveler ascended to the palaces. The chariot was inside the self as well as in the heavenly realms.

Because the tree uses the ten sephiroth and the twenty-two pathways we naturally think of it as derived from the Sefer Yetsirah and the work of creation. And of course it is, not just because of its structure but because of its tradition of contemplating the wonders of existence. But it also derives from the work of the chariot, for the tree is a vehicle as much as a thing of wonder. We use it not just to understand how life exists, or even how to understand divine laws; we use it to understand ourselves. And we use it to move ourselves through the journey of the pathways, step by step, until we discover our own vision, as much as we are able, of divine truth. And it is the special wonder of Hermann Haindl's painting that he shows this vehicle to be one truly of life and not just abstract thought.

When Haindl writes on his painting "der baum ist der baum ist der baum ist der baum" ("The tree is the tree is the tree is the tree," reminiscent of Gertrude Stein's legendary poem "A rose is a rose is a rose is a rose"), he returns the philosophical concept to its literal roots. Around the world we find the Tree of Life seen as an actual tree, alive in the world. In the West we have lost our connections to nature as a divine revelation so that we tend to think of spiritual ideas as apart from the living world. We even may see the two as opposed, with anything physical being temporary and ultimately empty, while the spiritual becomes the thought that transcends nature. The Haindl tree, however, reminds us that we exist in nature, and if we cannot find the divine in living things then perhaps we will find it nowhere.

In Africa and many other places, trees with white sap have signified the Mother Goddess, for they give "milk" yet, unlike short-lived humans, they remain strong and graceful over many decades, even centuries. Ancient Egypt identified the sycamore with the goddesses Nut (of the night sky, possibly the oldest goddess), Hathor (identified with the cow goddess), and Isis, founder of civilization, bringer of Osiris back from the dead.

Osiris himself becomes embedded in a tree at one point of his story. His brother Set imprisons him in a jeweled coffin and floats him away down the Nile. The coffin drifts out to sea and lands at a place called Byblos, where a tree grows up around it to become the base of the local king's palace. Isis finds him and removes him from the tree. Osiris's ceremonies included the raising of a wooden pole called the Djed pillar, a symbol both of the male organ with its generative power and the human backbone, the structure that allows us to stand upright—like a tree—and move in the world. The backbone contains the life energy people in India call *kundalini*, sometimes thought of as a snake coiled at the base of the spine.

The image of a snake wound around a tree recalls the Tree of Life in the Garden of Eden, and also the common image of healing from the Greek caduceus, two snakes wound around a stick (now a symbol of the medical profession). And, further, it may remind us of the "brazen serpent" that God tells Moses to hold before the Israelites as they travel in the wilderness. This, too, was said to heal the sick. The more we delve into the symbolism and myths of different cultures—in this case, Egypt, India, Israel, and Greece, but we could cite even more—the more we realize that myths and esoteric teachings are not fantasies or even just psychological insights, but are in fact ways to represent scientific knowledge that the modern world has largely lost.

Even in ancient Israel, people saw the Tree of Life as a real tree. Most often this was the almond, a tree whose white flowers bloomed early in spring, before its first leaves. The oil cups in sacred menorahs (candleholders) were often shaped like almond flowers. The menorahs themselves took on the form of a tree, with seven branches, one for each of the days of creation, and ultimately for each of the seven moving bodies in the sky—sun, moon, Mercury, Venus, Mars, Jupiter, and Saturn. These seven bodies were the source of the seven palaces of heaven, the hekhaloth.

Long before he learned of the Kabbalah Tree of Life, Hermann Haindl witnessed a living ritual of this idea. For a number of years, he and his wife Erica were privileged to attend the annual Native American Sun Dance, in which various Indian nations come together in a great ritual of sacrifice and celebration. Young men, who have prepared themselves for an entire year, pierce their bodies and dance about a tree, offering their own blood, like sap from a tree, to strengthen what the great visionary Black Elk called the "sacred hoop" that connects all life. Interestingly, they perform the ritual around a sapling, not some ancient tree older than memory. The Tree of Life ultimately is all trees, and the youngest shoot reaches into the roots of the very beginnings of life.

To offer blood means to offer yourself, to break the barrier of skin that seems to separate you from the universe outside you. "The blood is the life," says the Bible. The young men in the ceremony do not die or injure themselves in any permanent way. The blood sacrifice does not seek harm but a union with the natural and spiritual worlds.

Black Elk described many sacred hoops for the many peoples of the world. And yet they all form one great circle. Black Elk also spoke of a single great tree, flowering and beautiful, that shelters all the children of the earth. Similarly, the Revelation of St. John describes a Tree of Life with twelve fruits (for the twelve signs of the zodiac) that yields every month, and branches whose leaves shelter and heal all the nations of humanity. Both these visions describe the tree's nurturing powers, compared to the Kabbalist or shamanic vision of a kind of ladder that links heaven, earth, and the underworld. Because Hermann Haindl's painting shows the tree so vibrantly alive, it combines both these qualities, the nurturance and the vision of the laws of creation.

The Sun Dance brings to mind two mythological tree sacrifices of great importance to European traditions. The first is Jesus on the cross, the second is the Norse/Germanic god Odin, who hangs from the world tree, Yggdrasil, to obtain the magical alphabet, the runes.

Christian teachings specifically compare the cross to the Tree of Life denied Adam and Eve in the Garden of Eden (we will look more closely at the Eden story in a moment). Just as some stories say that Jesus himself made the cross in his work as a carpenter, so others claim the wood literally came from the original Tree of Life. The first humans disobeyed the Creator and ate from the Tree of Knowledge, losing Paradise for all humanity. Christ gives up his own life and then returns from the dead to redeem humanity from sin. Christian myth not only links the cross to the Tree of Life, it also links Christ's sacrifice to Abraham's willingness to sacrifice Isaac, for Calgary, the hill where Christ died, is said to be the same place where Abraham bound Isaac and prepared to offer him to God, until an angel came and told him to sacrifice a ram instead. Jewish Kabbalah considers Isaac the embodiment of the fourth sephirah, Chesed, or mercy.

As we have seen, Christian (also Western) Kabbalah places Christ in the center of the tree, at the sixth sephirah, Tiferet. Just as we can think of the entire tree as a human body, so we also can visualize Christ at the center, suspended on the cross. (We should recognize here that the Haindl painting actually shows Christ, with his crown of thorns, on the right pillar of the tree. This is the pillar of mercy, and so a fitting place for the image of a savior. The center sephirah in the Haindl tree shows a bird. For Christians, this suggests the Holy Spirit.)

Some scholars believe that the Romans did not actually use crosses for execution but instead nailed people to simple poles (the word *crucifix* comes from Latin and means "fixed to a cross," but *crucifixion* may not be the original term). If so, Christianity adopted the image of Christ as nailed to a cross for two reasons. First, the cross allows the human body to open up, with the arms out expansively, as if to embrace all humanity. Christ's body becomes more like a tree, a protective shelter.

Second, the cross forms a powerful symbol of the intersection between eternity and history. In other words, the vertical line of the cross represents the divine, which is ever present, eternal, all powerful. The horizontal line signifies the historical moment and chain of events that led to Christ's sacrifice. Another way to say this is that the vertical line symbolizes Christ's divinity, while the horizontal line indicates Jesus's humanity.

We find the symbolism of the cross in other traditions beside Christianity. In both ancient Greek religion and Haitian Voudoun, divinities appear at crossroads that symbolize the meeting place of different realities, especially that of gods and humans.

Though Christian Kabbalah places Christ in the center of the tree, the entire Tree of Life represents a meeting, or junction, of human history and divinity. This is because it begins with an image of eternity, in Kether, and reaches down to what we think of as "the real world" in Malkuth.

This movement goes both ways. If we think of the tree as the process of creation, then the energy moves from Kether, sephirah one, down the Tree to Malkuth, sephirah ten. But we also can think of the tree as a pathway for us to return to divine awareness. We can imagine ourselves moving up the tree, from Malkuth to Kether. And if we think of the tree as a model for our own bodies, then we can allow energy to awaken in us and rise upwards, from Malkuth at our feet to Kether at the top of our heads. Such movement can transform our ordinary view of existence, which we might call "mortal," into an awareness of our eternal "true" selves, at one with the divine life energy that never dies.

The story of Odin's sacrifice so recalls Christ that early myth and folklore researchers assumed the Norse writers had borrowed it from Christianity. Since then, most have agreed that the story is much older than the Christian presence in the north. It may go back to very ancient practices in Siberia of sacrificing horses (similar to the sacrifice of bulls in ancient Greece or, for that matter, rams in ancient Israel). In the myth, Odin had a horse named Ygg, and the name of the tree, Yggdrasil, may have meant "steed of Odin."

The essence of the tree is renewal. Like serpents who shed their skin and emerge reborn—like the moon, which grows strong, then dies into darkness only to remerge once more into light—(deciduous) trees shed their leaves as the earth goes cold in winter, then returns to life in spring. According to Norse myth a great battle called Ragnarok will destroy the gods and all life. Yggdrasil itself will shatter, breaking the link between all the worlds. Only—the tree secretly contains a future man and woman, and when the old Tree of Life dies these two will stand revealed to await the renewal of creation, like a new Adam and Eve.

Odin seeks the knowledge and magical power hidden in the runes, which lie in a dark well at the base of the World Tree. To prepare himself, he wounds himself in the side and then hangs on the tree for nine days and nights. Even this is not enough, and so he gives up his right eye as an offering to Mimir, the ruler of the well. Finally, Odin reaches down from the tree and snatches up the runes. Because of Odin's status as father of the gods, Western Kabbalah places Odin at the second sephirah, Hokhmah, identified with the "supernal father." *Hokhmah* means "wisdom," and having achieved the runes Odin became a master of true wisdom, someone who can see into all the worlds.

The runes resemble the Hebrew alphabet, for they spell words like any letters and yet they also contain special powers and symbolic meanings. We can use both alphabets for divination, and in very similar ways. The diviners would inscribe the letters on small stones or pieces of wood, put these in a bag and shake them, then reach inside for one or more letters to answer a question.

In both the Futhark (runes) and the Aleph-Beth (Hebrew), every letter describes some creature or quality. For example, the third Hebrew letter, Gimel, means "camel," while the rune Ur means "aurochs," a European bison (extinct since the Middle Ages). Both letters, Gimel (ג) and Ur (ᚢ), appear on Hermann Haindl's painting of the High Priestess Tarot card.

The Sefer Yetsirah describes the Creation as the product of the ten sephiroth and the twenty-two Hebrew letters. The Kabbalah Tree of Life brilliantly combines these two in the diagram of twenty-two pathways connecting the sephiroth. Nineteenth-century Western Kabbalists then linked the letters and pathways to the twenty-two letters of the Major Arcana of the Tarot. In the Haindl tree painting we find the names of these cards on the lines between the sephiroth, while the actual Haindl Tarot cards also contain runes so that we could, in fact, use them to place the runes on the tree.

TWO

The Tree *Within the* Tree

We have already glimpsed the many sources, ideas, and symbols that go into the diagram of the Kabbalah Tree of Life. The most obvious source, however, remains the story of Adam and Eve and the Garden of Eden. We are going to spend some time with this account, partly because its subtleties illuminate the tree in important ways, and partly because it can teach us how to look at myths and the kind of images that populate Hermann Haindl's painting.

Most Western people think they know this story. God tells Adam and Eve not to eat the apple, the serpent gets Eve to try it, she gives some to Adam, God banishes them from the garden, and humanity has suffered ever since. Christians call this the Fall, the source of what St. Augustine called "original sin," by which everyone alive, as the descendants of Adam and Eve, shares their sinful state. Christ's sacrifice on the cross supposedly redeems humanity and saves it from hell. This is why Christian myth describes the cross as literally made from the Tree of Life.

The story, however, is a great deal more subtle than it seems. Because of its importance to the Kabbalist vision we will look at it more closely. We also will see how Hermann Haindl's own vision gains meaning from the story of Eden.

Just as the Jews originally thought of the Tree of Life as an actual tree, so they considered Eden a genuine place in the world. The Bible tells us that a river ran through Eden, and as it left it split into four rivers, including the Tigris and Euphrates that nurtured the early Middle Eastern civilization of Babylon (now Iraq). This gives us an example of the way the myth of the Tree of Life works, for as we shall see in chapter three, the Kabbalah teaches that in fact there is not one tree but four. The Creator did not form the world all at once. Instead, God made *four* worlds, each one progressively more solid. Just as the single river in the garden changes to four actual rivers in the ordinary world, so the original power of the divine expresses itself in the four worlds. Myth and reality become one.

The word *Eden* is originally Sumerian (the culture that preceded Babylon). It first meant a place that was once lush but became barren. Later, it came to mean an uncultivated steppe, or hinterland. When human consciousness dwells within the place of origin, the place of the Tree of Life, then it keeps its character as a lush garden. But when human consciousness goes into exile, when we lose the sense of who we really are, the garden becomes wild and even barren. This radical idea—that the perfection of divine creation requires human consciousness—is partly what the story means when it says that God created the garden, and then set the human inside to tend it and to keep watch over it.

We often hear the Garden of Eden referred to as "Paradise." This word actually comes later, when people had begun to see the lost home in more otherworldly terms. The Hebrew word for paradise is very close, *pardes*. It actually means an orchard—that is, a beautiful garden of fruitful trees. One of the most important Kabbalist texts was called the "Orchard of Pomegranates." Paradise originally comes from a Persian word, *paradeiza*, meaning "an enclosed space," like a cultivated garden or orchard protected from the harsh world.

In Hebrew (and Arabic, the language of the Qur'an), letters are all consonants, with vowel sounds added underneath the letters—or simply implied. If we wrote English this way, the word "word" would appear as "WRD." This quality takes on great importance in Kabbalah, for two words with the same consonants become the same, with only the context to make it clear which word belongs in a sentence. This allows us to discover powerful connections between words. Again, with an English example, we would notice that "God" and "good" and "guide" are all spelled "GD." For this reason, Jews and Muslims will often say that the Hebrew Bible and the Qur'an cannot truly be translated, for the words lose all the extra dimensions that come with their connections to other words with the same letters. (Another form of Kabbalist word connection, called gematria, comes from the fact that every Hebrew letter is also a number. This makes it possible to add up the number value of any word and link it to other words with the same number value.)

Kabbalah depends greatly on these kinds of connections. They allow us to look inside the tree and other symbols to discover many layers of possible meaning. Hermann Haindl's painting, by adding layers of imagery, gives us a visual quality of many dimensions similar to the traditional Kabbalist use of word connections.

Among all these word plays, paradise—PRDS, since we only write the consonants—carries a special meaning. First, the fact that it has four letters marks it as unusual, for most Hebrew (or Arabic) words have roots of three letters. Four letters for the word *paradise* immediately suggests the four worlds of Kabbalah, but also God's most holy name in the Bible, often called the tetragrammaton, because it also contains four letters. In Kabbalistic thought there is not one reality but four. The worlds move between the poles of the spiritual and the physical, with our world of "action," the fourth world (Assiyah), being furthest from the more spiritual world of the "archetypal" first world of "emanation" (Atzilut). Kabbalists usually visualize the four worlds vertically, by extending the Jacob's ladder quality of the tree so that we get four trees overlapping each other, with the top of each lower tree becoming the bottom of the one above it. Such an image ultimately derives from that idea of ascent and descent, the climb up to heaven or down to earth. (These ideas will become clearer in the following chapter, when we explore the four worlds more fully.)

But we also can look at the four worlds in another way, as each one embedded within the other. At any point, we really exist in all four worlds at once; we just have not learned how to look through the surfaces to see the layers inside. We have not really *lost* paradise; we just have lost the ability to *recognize* it. The four letters of PRDS give us four ways of seeing: the practical, the intellectual, the allegorical, and the mystical. Paradise is not just one of these—not just the mystical experience of the divine—but *all* of these, for we need all four letters to spell the word.

So it is with the Tree of Life, or the four trees of the four worlds. We are not really stuck down here in Malkuth of Assiyah—that is, in the lowest emanation of the lowest tree. That is just our limited vision. We exist within the entire tree, and the entire tree exists within us. Once again, Hermann Haindl's painting allows us to glimpse this, for it shows us layers of imagery all at once, from the very direct pictures of a bird or a smiling mouth, to more subtle, harder to grasp qualities, to allegorical or mythic figures, to the abstract form of the pure tree.

The rabbis of the early Kabbalah (and the chariot mysticism that preceded it) used the four letters of PRDS as a guideline for interpreting the sacred text, the Torah, which they considered divinely written. To truly understand the Torah would mean to dwell in Paradise. Since we might say the same for the Tree of Life—to truly understand it, on all four levels, not just as a concept, would bring us to the divine—we can learn how to look at the tree from the four-letter method of interpretation.

PRDS becomes an acrostic, that is, each letter represents a word, and a way to understand what we read (or see). P stands for *peshat*, the literal level of interpretation. The Hebrew word means "plain, simple." We cannot just treat everything as symbolic, or consider the ordinary world as an illusory fake. Imagine a bumper sticker for a car: "Reality is real. That's why we call it reality." R means *remez*, Hebrew for "wink, hint, allusion." This represents the more intellectual approach and the first level of metaphor. D stands for *drash*, an "exposition, sermon, homily." This is the allegorical level, in which the metaphors become much fuller and complete. For this level of interpretation the rabbis often developed elaborate stories called *midrashim* (plural of *midrash*), based upon characters and scenes from the Bible. In a sense, the entire imagery of the Tree of Life is a midrash from the story of Adam and Eve in Eden.

Finally, S means *sod*, or "secret." This is the secret or mystical meaning of any sacred story or image. We cannot understand this level through ordinary means, but must approach it through intuition and a sense of inner truth. At the same time, and paradoxically, it is often the literal statements or pictures that most direct us to the mystical. The picture of the Tree of Life is provocative and mysterious. To look at it gives us a glimpse of its deeper truths. We feel that tingle of excitement, that sense of wonder and awe we experience when we hear an ancient myth. It is this excitement that leads us to the mystical level of the tree. We need the intellectual and symbolic levels to get there, for we need to grasp what it all means. But if we believe that the concepts are all that matter, then we will never enter that state of paradise that comes from true understanding. P-R-D-S is not a line but a circle, and in a circle the P and S touch each other.

To put it another way, if we take away the P and the S, all we have left is R & D, research and development. We may get the intellectual development of the tree; we may even get some practical uses from it. For example, we may see how we can use the tree in rituals or magic. We may learn to use it as a symbol for something like neural pathways in the brain. But we will have lost the story, and without that we will never find our way to that mystic understanding that is the real purpose of the entire tree.

My friend Zoe Matoff, who thinks deeply about such matters, has suggested that we can actually map these four letters/levels onto the tree itself. If we place the P in Malkuth, the sephirah that represents the physical world, and S in Kether, the sephirah closest to the divine, that leaves

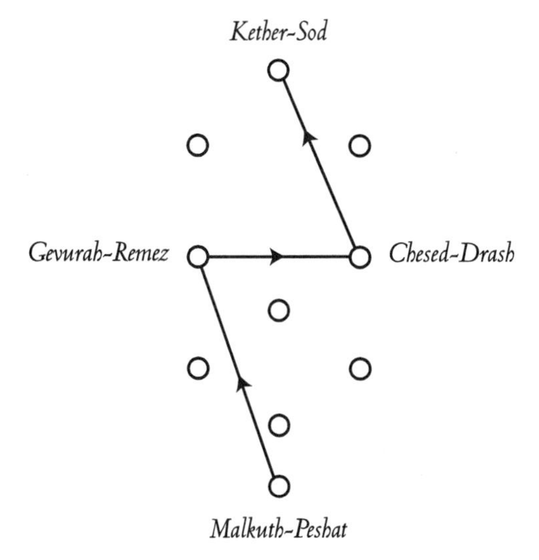

the R and the D for the two pillars on the sides. Perhaps the pillar of justice, on the left, would contain remez, the intellectual level, and mercy, on the right, contain drash, the allegorical. We can be more specific and place remez in Gevurah and drash in Chesed, for these two sephiroth, power and mercy, epitomize the two pillars. In this way, the four levels of interpreting a story or image become a means of traveling up the tree to spiritual awareness, from Malkuth to Gevurah to Chesed to Kether.

With that in mind, let us return to the peshat—the story—of the Garden of Eden.

Genesis actually gives us two versions of the Creation. In the first, which gives the famous "six days" account, no mention is made of Eden or the two trees. Nor does it describe Eve as created from Adam's rib. Instead, it describes the different stages over the days, ending with the creation of humanity. Male and female come into being together, on the sixth day, without names.

The phrase used for this creation is very important in Kabbalah. "Male and female, He created them," the text tells us. Even before the development of Kabbalistic ideas, the ancient rabbis noticed that this phrase "male and female" does not only describe the first humans, it describes God. This is because in Hebrew as well as in English, an introductory phrase in a sentence grammatically refers to the next noun or pronoun. In other words, in that sentence, "Male and female, He created them," the words "male and female" refer to "He," God. From this we can understand God as hermaphroditic, with both masculine and feminine aspects.

On a deeper level than grammar, if humans exist "in God's image" (the expression appears just before "male and female . . ."), then both women and men reflect the divine essence of our Creator, who must also contain both qualities—despite the constant use of the word "He." In fact, some of the words used to describe God in the Bible have their root in the female body, and so are actually Goddess terms. For example, the biblical word for mercy, or merciful, derives from the word for womb. *Shaddai*, a biblical word often translated as "Almighty," actually comes from a word that means breasts.

The Kabbalists developed this idea of the hermaphroditic God much further. From these issues we get the concept that the Tree of Life con-

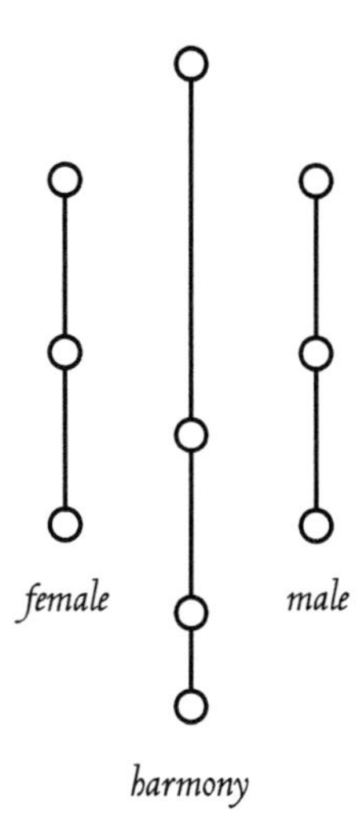

tains male and female pillars (the vertical columns on the right and left), and the need to reconcile them.

We also get the concept that the female aspect of God, the Shekhinah, dwells in Malkuth. We will look at these ideas more closely, and how we can use them with the tree and, more importantly, in our lives, in later chapters.

No prohibitions appear in this first chapter of Genesis. God tells them that they may treat all creatures as food, with no restrictions, and describes the land as "having a soul" (Genesis 1:30). God also tells them to be fertile and populate the earth.

The familiar account of the garden, and the rib, appears in chapter two. And here, humans do not appear at the very end of Creation, but towards the beginning. The book tells us that God made heaven and earth, but no plants existed, for God had not created rain to moisten the ground (remember that this story comes from the Middle East, where life depended on the rainy seasons) or man to work the soil. So God creates a mist to water the earth, and then shapes man out of the dirt. The name Adam comes from "ground," *adamah* in Hebrew, but also *adom*, "red," and *dam*, "blood."

Only after the creation of Adam does God "plant a garden in Eden, to the east" (Genesis 2:8). The story goes on to tell us that every tree grew there, including, in the center of the garden, the Tree of Life and the Tree of Knowledge of Good and Evil. It then goes on to describe Eden's geography, and the four rivers, and after that, how God puts Adam in the garden "to work it and watch it" (Genesis 2:15). But now God adds a warning. Eat of everything else, the Creator says, but not from the Tree of Knowledge. "Eat from it, and on that day you will definitely die" (Genesis 2:17).

Notice that the prohibition does not include the Tree of Life. Does this mean that they could eat from that tree so long as they didn't eat from knowledge? Or could it mean that without knowledge they somehow didn't know about it? These questions are crucial to understanding the Kabbalah tree and just what it means. We will come back to these issues in a moment.

Now God decides that Adam needs a helper of some kind. The text goes on to say that God "formed every wild beast and every bird of heaven out of the ground" (Genesis 2:19). Remember that this was how the Creator made Adam. We can take this to mean that even though humanity may possess a consciousness beyond those of animals, we all come from the same source—the earth. Contrary to what a lot of people believe, Genesis shows an ecological understanding that all of life comes from "the ground," and so all of life is related. God originally set Adam in the garden to tend it, to help the plants grow and to watch over them. After many centuries of an ideology that teaches the world lies there for us to exploit it, it is useful to discover that the Bible actually teaches something very different.

It also helps us understand the Tree of Life and what it can mean to us. Does it separate us from the physical world? Does it lift us away from the material into a disembodied spiritual state? Certainly some people interpret it that way, but I do not think it requires us to approach it with such ideas in mind. Instead, we can think of the tree as a means to recover our understanding of life's web of connections. Again, the Haindl imagery of a tree filled with actual life—human, animal, plant, and suggestions of spirits—helps remind us of Eden as a place to feel all life joined together.

So all the creatures come before Adam, as if to audition for the role of companion. Instead, Adam names them; in fact, part of God's purpose in this parade of creatures was curiosity "to see what he would name each one" (trans. Aryeh Kaplan). Language distinguishes us from animals. It does not necessarily give us power over other beings—the text says nothing about Adam gaining any magical control through these names—but it does help form our gift of consciousness. As many people have noted, this gift is also dangerous, for it can separate us from the actual experience and wonder of creation. If we look at a huge plant that grows from the ground and just think the word "tree," we lose the reality.

And yet language is part of our deepest nature. To attempt to deny it would be to deny our humanity. We need to use language, the desire and ability to name things so that we will understand and remember them, as a path to experience the deeper levels of existence. This need belongs to the Kabbalah tree, especially the Western Hermetic version, with all its complex correspondences. We comprehend the sephiroth partly through learning their many attributes. We can think of this as an extension of Adam's ability to name the creatures. And, in fact, Kabbalah tradition teaches us that the doctrines originated in Eden with a secret book revealed to Adam and preserved through the millennia, until the time came to write these things down and reveal them to the world.

Now we come to one of the most famous scenes, that notorious rib. Since none of the beasts can really serve Adam as a companion, God puts Adam into a deep sleep, a kind of trance, and removes a rib. Out of this rib the Creator creates a woman. From this story generations of men have tried to prove women's inferiority. St. Paul said that women should not speak in church but let their husbands speak for them, because God made woman from man. But if we return to the peshat, the literal account, we find no such statement. Instead, we learn that a man must leave his parents and "cleave" to his wife, "and they shall become one flesh."

But what happens when we go beyond the literal? What lessons can we find from this account once we get over the political arguments about whether it makes women inferior? Here we come to that radical interpretation that both God and the original human were hermaphroditic, "male and female" not as separate beings, but one creation.

This perfect being contained all qualities, both masculine and feminine. One thing it could not do, however, was discover new things about itself through dialogue with someone else. It existed alone, perfect in itself, but without a partner. And so the Creator separated it into two parts, each one whole in her- or himself but a complement to the other.

And because these humans come in the image of God, we can say the same thing about the divine. In other words, God's true nature is hermaphroditic, but without a partner God cannot fully know his/her own divinity. To those who grew up in religious traditions that assumed God knows everything, this idea may sound very radical, and certainly outside Western beliefs. It may sound more Pagan, where God and Goddess are honored. But one aspect of Kabbalah is its fearlessness, and the willingness to follow where the truth seems to lead.

In Kabbalah, the universe exists just because God wished a reflection of self. When the divine power emerged into the tree—that is, into a universe—a male and female aspect developed into those right and left pillars. The separation of Adam and Eve who, after all, were made in God's image, reflects the split in the divine.

These ideas imply the great importance of humans to creation. Rather than being insignificant, empty creatures compared to God's powers, humans first of all demonstrate the actual state of divinity, for we are in God's image. And humans can take an active role in harmonizing and restoring the separated aspects of God.

Hermann Haindl's tree painting implies restoration through the ancientness of its pictures, a quality Haindl calls "archaic," or original, from the first existence before all the many details and conflicts of cultures separated us from our basic sense of life. This archaic quality pervades all of Haindl's work. In his earlier paintings, in his Tarot cards, and now in the tree, we find this ancientness over and over—trees so old they look like stone; rocks so old they have softened into faces; animals, like swans or bulls, that people have seen as sacred all over the world. When we contemplate the Haindl tree we get the chance to explore, each to our own level, the layers of meaning in the sephiroth and their paths. But we also get a chance to sense a return to our own origins.

Kabbalah teaches us to look on nature as an opening. We see into nature and through it to the divine essence that fills all of existence, the sephiroth within the outer profusion of life. This is what science tries to do, study the myriad wonders of the natural world and find patterns and laws. Many people see Kabbalah as a kind of science, informed by divine inspiration as well as analysis and investigation. And many scientists will recognize that the steps of PRDS—literal observation, intellectual context, greater patterns, laws of nature—form a perfect representation of their own work.

We can describe our usual lack of awareness in terms of the tree itself. Malkuth, the bottom sephirah, represents the outer form of existence. If we look at the world and see only what's in front of us, if we don't look deeper to what lies beyond, then we see Malkuth alone and ignore all the sephiroth that have fed into it. We cannot move up the tree if we do not recognize its existence. And this indeed is how some Kabbalists describe Adam's great sin.

The original human, the reflection of the divine, looked on the tree and mistook the beauty of Malkuth for all existence. Because of this, Adam lost the tree and separated into male and female halves. But each of us has the possibility to restore the wholeness, to heal the world.

There are many myths and radical ideas in Kabbalah, just as in the world's religions, and some of these may seem to contradict each other. We should not worry too much about this, for each interpretation reveals some aspect of truth. To try to get a single "correct" interpretation is similar to thinking that Malkuth is all of existence. Thus we can see the creation of Eve out of Adam's side as a primal separation. But we also can see the emergence of Eve as the completion of Adam, the final step.

Like everyone else, the great Kabbalists—and indeed the Bible writers before them—were limited by culture. Because they came from a patriarchal society they looked on the separation between male and female and saw the male as primary. Eve must come out of Adam. Science—and the very oldest myths—suggest the opposite, that in evolutionary terms the male emerged from the female. The earliest organisms reproduced by the "mother" splitting into two "daughters" exactly identical to the original. The separation into two sexes made it possible for new creatures to come into existence, for in sexual reproduction the mother and father combine their genes to produce a child unique and original.

With Adam and Eve the garden becomes complete. Or perhaps we should say "ready," for the seeming perfection of Paradise really just sets the stage. Stability is not the way of the world, change is. Tell a child the story without giving it the weight of religious doctrine. "There were once a man and woman who came to live in a beautiful garden. The owner of the garden told them 'You can do whatever you like, enjoy everything, I just don't want you to take any apples from this one tree.'" And then say to the child, "What do you think happens next?" The child will laugh and say, "They take the apple!"

Of course, in the Bible they don't just do it, another actor enters the scene. The Bible calls the serpent "cunning," and implies an evilness in its intentions. Some snakes, of course, are poisonous, and so we need to fear or at least respect them. Some Christian fundamentalists teach that Satan inhabited the snake, and some Jews say the same about Samael, the medieval Jewish name for an Evil One. But the Bible says nothing about this.

The serpent is a much more complex figure than the story suggests. We might guess this by the fact that one way for our consciousness to move up the Kabbalah tree bears the title "the Way of the Serpent," in which we entwine ourselves from sephirah ten to nine to eight and so on up to one. If we look at Hermann Haindl's painting we find a large snake around the fourth sephirah, Chesed (middle right) and a group of three snakes around Gevurah (middle left). Haindl painted them there for the deep significance of serpents the world over, an example of that "archaic" symbolism so important to his artistic vision.

Snakes fascinate us. They move so quickly, without legs, like sensual lightning. The essentially phallic form suggests male sexuality, but the way they coil and fold around themselves hints at the complexity of the vulva. Snakes grow by periodically shedding their skins (about the time I began this book I found a shed snakeskin just outside my back door) so that they suggest immortality. People who have face-lifts and other plastic surgery to appear young again are trying to imitate the serpent.

The Eden story contains one snake and two trees. In Greek myth the God Hermes (the Western Kabbalah tradition is called "hermetic") creates a magical healing staff of two serpents wound around one stick. This "caduceus," as the Greeks called it, still appears as the symbol of the medical profession. So, mythologically, a snake can poison us, but snakes also can heal us.

The human body itself is a kind of caduceus. The tradition of yoga describes the basic life energy, called kundalini, as a snake coiled at the base of the spine. But when the energy awakens, the description changes to two streams of snakelike energy, called ida and pingala, that wind around the spine like Hermes' caduceus.

Is this idea—and the Way of the Serpent—only a fancy metaphor? The venom of certain snakes can produce visions similar to the sacred trances brought on by peyote or various mushrooms. Shamans and others will extract the venom and take it in measured doses, or else build up an immunity by careful exposure to the bites so that a larger bite will bring visions rather than injury.

People interpret the snake's action, and the loss of Paradise, in different ways from their different points of view. Christians speak of a "fortunate fall," for if humans had stayed innocent, in an earthly paradise, there would have been no cause for Christ to redeem them to a higher existence. Modern Goddess worshippers see the garden as originally the place of a goddess and her companion snake. Indeed, in Canaan, and well into the time of ancient Israel, the goddess Asherah was worshiped in groves of trees. We might remember here that the Hebrew word *pardes* means "orchard." In this myth, then, the goddess freely gives her fruit of eternal life to her initiates, aided by her vision-inducing serpent. The story of Eden becomes a veiled reference to the patriarchal Hebrews' destruction of the goddess religion (for more on this interpretation, see *Occidental Mythology* by Joseph Campbell, *When God Was a Woman* by Merlin Stone, and my own *The Body of the Goddess*).

The Kabbalist interpretation of the snake and the forbidden fruit is both subtle and complex. It involves the mysteries of exile and return, innocence and awareness. To understand these issues, we will return to the peshat, the story as it appears in Genesis.

The cunning serpent first asks Eve, "Did God really tell you not to eat from any of the trees?" Oh no, Eve says, they can eat from all of them but that one. If they just touch it, they will die. Now, Eve has made a mistake here, for God did not say the tree was dangerous just to touch. A midrash story describes how the serpent saw his chance, and bumped Eve so that she touched the tree and he could say, "There. You see. You're all right." But the rabbis actually go further to make an interesting point. They absolve Eve of guilt on the grounds that Adam exaggerated the instructions to her, and so made her vulnerable. Zoe Matoff has pointed out to me that the real responsibility rests with God, for delegating the instruction job to Adam instead of telling Eve himself.

This technical absolution of Eve would not matter so much if not for the belief in Western culture that all of "man's" troubles come from woman. In terms of the two trees, what the serpent says next is most important. He tells Eve that the danger of death is not true, but God knows that if she eats of the Tree of Knowledge "your eyes will be opened, and you will be like God, knowing good and evil." Considering that indeed Eve and Adam do not die, and indeed they become aware of good and evil, is the serpent telling the truth?

There is a long esoteric tradition that considers the serpent the hero of the story. In this version the god of Genesis is a kind of tyrant who tries to keep humans ignorant of their true divine nature. The rebel serpent, who can symbolize the kundalini energy of the awakened spirit-body, tries to liberate Adam and Eve with the power of knowledge, called in Greek *gnosis*. The followers of this idea, called Gnostics, were the enemy of the early church. Though the Gnostics were often anti-semitic, Gershon Scholem, a great twentieth-century scholar of Kabbalist traditions, described Kabbalah as Jewish Gnosticism. Certainly the Western, or Christian, versions of Kabbalah borrow heavily from Gnostic ideas.

Eve eats from the apple, but nothing much seems to happen, not until she gives some to Adam. Once again, we find that need to complete the male and female, the same teaching shown in the right and left pillars of the tree. As soon as Adam joins her their eyes indeed are "opened." They do not die, but instead see . . . what? They see that they are naked.

The Hebrew word for "knowledge" in this story is *da'ath*. This same word appears on the Tree of Life as a hidden or "uncreated" sephirah in the space between the higher three sephiroth and the lower seven.

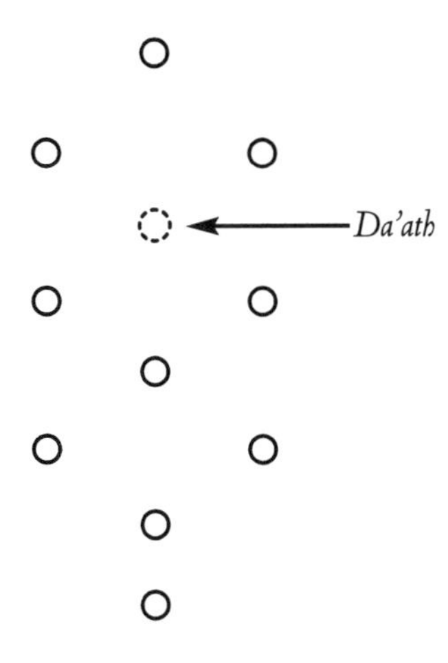

We will learn more about this hidden sephirah later, but right now, we should know that da'ath carries the connotation of sexuality, as in the famous biblical expression "He knew his wife." So the knowledge Adam and Eve get from the fruit somehow involves sex. Many people assume it is entirely sex, that Adam and Eve loved each other without carnal knowledge (that word again) until they ate from the tree. But the story does not support this idea, for back in the first version of creation, God tells "the male and female" to "be fertile and multiply."

No, the knowledge is not sex but shame about sex. We might think of it as the knowledge that separates us from our actions, so that we look at ourselves through accusing eyes. At the same time, notice that Adam and Eve do not die, as God had warned Adam. Instead, they lose their true spirit selves, perfectly in harmony, to a false knowledge that they are "naked." In this way they begin a path away from the divine and toward death. This is knowledge (Da'ath) without wisdom (sephirah two), knowledge without understanding (sephirah three). It comes from the single snake of cunning rather than the double snake of healing.

In their shame they literally hide from God, behind bushes, and when God confronts Adam, Adam says he heard God in the wind, and was ashamed to show himself naked—to which God says, "Who told you you were naked?" The secret is out.

Think about this. Kabbalist tradition teaches that just as the light enters the tree through Kether, the crown, so divine energy enters humans through the top of the head, what yoga calls the crown chakra. Jewish men wear *yarmulkes* (skullcaps) on top of their heads because they believe their bodies could not sustain the unfiltered energy coming to them from the divine. And this is simply the energy in its most dense form, coming from Malkuth, the bottom sephirah in the fourth world of creation. When Adam and Eve lived in the garden they lived in the presence of the entire Tree of Life and moved innocently through all its radiance. When they ate from knowledge—without wisdom or understanding—they became conscious of the devastating power for the first time. They felt naked, and afraid.

God then curses Adam and Eve and the snake in a series of denunciations that support the view of God as harsh. To some extent, these are what Rudyard Kipling called "just-so" stories, tales to explain phenomena about the world, such as the hard work it takes to grow food, or the agony of childbirth, or the fact that snakes move about without legs.

But now the story takes a startling turn. God speaks to what seems to be some unknown group. "Man has become like one of us in knowing good and bad. Now he must be prevented from also putting forth his hand and also taking from the Tree of Life. He can eat it and live forever!" First, this resembles what the serpent said. Is the serpent right? Did God just want to keep Adam and Eve ignorant? And is God just part of some group?

The Gnostics described the god of Genesis as an angel that wanted to become a creator. And so, the Gnostic myth goes, this Demiurge imprisoned souls in physical matter, and did everything possible to keep them from knowledge of their true state. When they learned part of the truth from the efforts of the snake, the Demiurge kept them from reaching out to the next part, the realization of their own bodiless perfection.

This interpretation is radical and challenging, and it can help us free ourselves from childhood religious training that treats the Eden story as historical fact. Ultimately, however, there is something pointless about seeing the Creator as a tyrant, and physical existence as a prison. Once we free ourselves from old guilt, where can we go with it? So let us try to do some further R & D (remez and drash) on the peshat of the Eden story, and see if it can point us to the sod, or secrets, of the tree, and especially the Haindl depiction of it.

Kabbalah teaches that all existence, as symbolized in the tree, originates from an En Sof, a nothingness that is one and eternal (for more on this term, see the following chapters). As the light emerged into Kether it stayed whole, but as it spilled down into the two pillars it took on aspects such as male and female, expansion and contraction. The creative power remains one, and we see this in the connection between the sephiroth. There is one tree—just as with an ordinary tree we see a trunk and branches and leaves and roots, but they all express different aspects of one organism.

Kabbalist texts describe the sephiroth directly under Kether in humanistic terms, as the "supernal father and mother" (Hokhmah and Binah, wisdom and understanding). The Zohar describes these very mythological figures as "a mystery of mysteries," with perhaps some worry that naïve readers might take such things as a literal description of a series of Pagan-like gods running the world.

In fact, most polytheistic religions, with their brilliant panoply of gods and goddesses, reflect the same idea as Kabbalah—that all the deities go back to a single divine energy that expressed itself in dramatic ways. In Hindu belief, existence and the gods stem from the vast unknowable energy called Brahman, and ultimately return to it after many millions of years. The Egyptians taught that the physical world and all the gods come from Atum, a figure beyond creation.

Western Kabbalah, with its synthesis of many cultures, goes beyond the Jewish tradition. In the center of the tree, Tiferet, they place not just Christ but the Egyptian Osiris and all the other dying and resurrected gods. Odin appears on the tree, and so do the Greek gods and planets of astrology. And on the Haindl tree we find animals and plants and stones and faces everywhere we look. And yet they all live on the tree.

Out of nothingness (the En Sof) comes one (Kether), out of one, two, and three (Hokhmah and Binah), and from the joining of two and three comes what Lao Tzu, the great Taoist sage, called (in the Tao Te Ching) "the ten thousand things," all the wondrous variety of creation. Remember that in the tree the En Sof generates Kether and Kether generates Hokhmah and Binah, and then below these three "supernal" sephiroth come the seven lower sephiroth of the knowable universe—the ten thousand things. The tree reminds us that we live in the world of the ten thousand, and we can use our knowledge of the sephiroth to grasp the way the world works. But we also can use the varied forms and qualities of the sephiroth as a way to try to recognize (re-cognize, bring back to awareness) the original energy, the One, that breathes through all existence.

Why does God tell the anonymous "we" that they need to stop Adam and Eve from reaching out to the Tree of Life now that they have eaten from the Tree of Knowledge? We can make an assumption here, based on the descriptions of Adam and Eve's shame. The "knowledge" they gain does not, in fact, reveal to them their true state, but separates them from it. Before they eat from da'ath, they live in a kind of unconscious harmony with their garden world. To leave that world puts them at the heart of a long journey that all humans must take. This is the journey of consciousness, which may take many lifetimes to fulfill. We can look at the Kabbalist tree as a map for that journey. If we do it, we do not return to innocence but instead come to something greater, a full awareness of our own perfect being.

Only—we cannot do it all at once. We cannot suddenly leap from Malkuth directly to Kether, for how could we sustain such power? And so we must leave our innocent Paradise and enter the world of struggle, with the tree and other sacred teachings to remind us that struggle alone does not define existence.

Adam and Eve eat from knowledge (da'ath) without understanding and wisdom (Binah and Hokhmah). We can think of analogues in our ordinary world. If da'ath indeed means sexuality, think of the people who express their sexuality with great power, and knowledge of techniques and seduction and control, but without the understanding of what it means or the wisdom to direct this wonderful life energy.

On a larger scale we can think of the destructive sides of technology, especially nuclear and other "highly advanced" weapons systems designed to kill vast numbers of people. The use of science to create such things gives us a perfect example of knowledge without understanding and wisdom. In an odd reflection of da'ath's suggestion of sexual knowledge, the engineers and scientists who worked on some of the complicated missile systems often described their work as "sexy." When the Manhattan Project exploded the first atomic bomb at Los Alamos, the scientists there passed around cigars with a band that read "It's a boy."

Finally, what of "religious" people who know right from wrong—that is, a set of fixed rules—but do not understand the real message of those rules, and lack the wisdom to apply them to actual life? In Ursula Le Guin's rendition of Lao Tzu (see further reading), "Obedience to law is the dry husk of loyalty and good faith" (ch. 38) and "In the degradation of the great way comes benevolence and righteousness" (ch. 18).

And yet the Way, the tree, remains. It continues to describe reality, to map the path through our struggles. Da'ath, the sephirah of knowledge, hides, for it lies in the abyss between the upper and lower worlds, between the supreme principles of being (the top three sephiroth) and the seven sephiroth below.

Did Adam and Eve eat from the Tree of Life before their fateful grab at knowledge? Some people say they ate unknowingly, without any sense of themselves as special or apart from the rest of the garden. If they had done as the Creator asked, and left knowledge—separation—alone, they would have lived forever. The warning that if they eat from da'ath "on that day" they will die becomes true in a subtle way, for they begin at that moment to die, even if it takes them some nine hundred years to get there.

There is another view of why God does not worry about Adam and Even and the Tree of Life until after they have eaten from knowledge. This interpretation, or drash, of the story (peshat) suggests that the problem did not come up before because they literally could not see the Tree of Life until they ate the fruit of knowledge and "their eyes were opened." The Tree of Life grew inside the Tree of Knowledge. Life is embedded in knowledge.

I confess I find this idea very appealing. It seems to epitomize the notion of an "esoteric" truth, for esoteric means what lies hidden inside the outer form of a teaching, the life that lies hidden in knowledge. I think of it as drash, the third level, rather than remez, the second, because it goes beyond the intellectual to a much wider view, and because it indeed seems to point to sod, the mystical wisdom hidden inside the story. Divine life lies inside knowledge, embedded in it, the way the four levels of

PRDS lie embedded in each other. If we can reach true knowledge, knowledge joined to understanding and wisdom, not separated from them, then indeed the full Tree of Life will stand revealed before us, with no barrier, or abyss, to separate the higher and lower principles.

Adam and Eve were not historical figures. They represent a state of being in which we grab at partial knowledge and end up separating ourselves from the very things we desire. We find we know enough to be ashamed and self-conscious, but not enough to be able to use our knowledge in a way that brings us closer to our deepest possibilities. We become exiled from our true selves and no longer remember who we really are.

But what will bring us back? On the tree, Da'ath, knowledge, becomes a hidden sephirah, concealed in the abyss. In other words, knowledge becomes embedded inside the Tree of Life. This is the opposite of Eden. There, life was embedded in knowledge; here, in the existence that we think of as the real world, knowledge is embedded in life. What does this mean? For one thing, it reminds us that as we live our lives, go about our business, struggle through sickness, and go through the joys and pains of love and family, every moment and action contain "secret" knowledge. The knowledge is secret, esoteric, because we usually cannot see the inner truth of what happens. Most of the time we do not even fully recognize our own motives and purposes. We act from conditioning, and fear, and cultural biases. And yet, at every instant, if we could just see the hidden meanings of things, the wonders of our true state would stand revealed. No vengeful God bars us from this knowledge. If we suddenly saw the complete truth, it would overwhelm us. And so we go about our lives in ignorance.

Da'ath lies hidden in the tree but, in fact, the Kabbalah Tree of Life, the whole tree, is all about knowledge. The deceptively simple diagram codes thousands of years of thought, meditation, and study. The Kabbalist masters who created it poured all their study and insights into it. The tree gives us the knowledge of all those great teachers who pondered and wrote about it and passed on their knowledge from one generation to another. Then what remains hidden?

Possibly Da'ath represents actual practices used to travel across the barriers between the lower and higher levels of awareness. The Hebrew word *da'ath* carries the suggestion of sexuality, and in many traditions, especially Hindu Tantra, and Gnosticism, people have used sexual magic as a way to transform the kundalini energy from simple physical desire to spiritual enlightenment. In the twentieth century, Aleister Crowley taught the importance of sex magic and was strongly condemned by the more puritan upholders of the Western Kabbalah tradition.

There may, however, be a much older example. People who read the Bible are sometimes shocked to find just how openly erotic the Song of Songs is. When the rabbis gathered, nearly two thousand years ago, to decide which books would form the official canon of the Bible, it was a man named Rabbi Akiva ben Joseph who argued for inclusion of the Song of Songs. According to the history that has come down to us, he described it as an allegory of God's love for his people Israel (Christians changed this to God's love for the church). Perhaps there was a more esoteric reason. Akiva was a mystic as well as a founder of the rabbinical tradition and a political leader. He helped develop the "merkavah" or chariot tradition of deep meditation and other exercises to make what we call shamanic journeys to the heavenly realms. Sexual magic may have been a part of this.

Some fourteen centuries later, Isaac Luria, a great Kabbalah teacher who developed much of the tradition around the Tree of Life, taught the importance of sexual love as a way to restore the male and female aspects of God. Men and women (this was a very heterosexual as well as patriarchal tradition) should make love on the night of the Sabbath not simply for physical pleasure but with the awareness that they act as vehicles for the divine restoration. When Adam and Eve ate so blindly from the tree of da'ath, they violated that awareness. If da'ath means sexuality, they used it only for gratification and so separated themselves from the divine. They even caused the divine itself to separate into male and female halves in exile from each other. To use the power of sexual magic just for pleasure and ego satisfaction is indeed dangerous, and so, in the story, God prevents Adam and Eve from reaching out to snatch the fruit from the Tree of Life. But da'ath still remains, even if hidden from those not ready to understand it. If we can use it properly it will (re)open the path back to the highest levels of consciousness.

We can say one thing more about the concealed knowledge in the Tree of Life. By bringing the tree so vividly alive, Hermann Haindl reveals a different kind of hidden knowledge, that the tree really is about life itself, in all its mystery. At the same time, his painting refutes the Gnostic belief that the physical world is some kind of prison. Instead, the world becomes the vehicle to reveal the sacred wonder that lies within every creature, every rock, every moment.

THREE

The History *of an* Image

Despite the claims of some devotees of the Tree of Life, its history is not eternal. Like all symbols, it grew over time, from human attempts to describe powerful understandings about the nature of God and creation, and our human involvement with both. The great historian and magician, Israel Regardie, wrote (in *The Garden of Pomegranates*) that the tree does not show absolute reality but functions as "the most convenient system . . . of classifying the phenomena of the Universe and recording their relations." Charles Poncé, in his book *Kabbalah*, writes that the tree is not really specific to any religious doctrine but shows us how the psychic self emerges from "whatever stands before the psyche—the Self, the Atman, the En Sof, or the divine prime mover under any other appellation."

The idea of the ten sephiroth goes back as much as eighteen hundred years to the Sefer Yetsirah—the Book of Formation (Yetsirah is the name of the third of the four worlds, though this idea does not appear until the twelfth century CE). Along with the intense meditative practices of the merkavah, or chariot, the Sefer Yetsirah forms the beginning of the mystical tradition later called Kabbalah. For some time the two paths seemed to compete with each other—the contemplative, called Ma'aseh Bereshith, or Work of Creation (*Bereshith* is the first word of Genesis, usually translated as "In the beginning"), and the more active, called Ma'aseh

Merkavah. Though the Tree of Life mostly comes from the contemplative tradition, it really brings the two together because the framework it creates allows us the possibility to travel the pathways.

The anonymous author of the Sefer Yetsirah (some attribute it to Akiva) described the world as made of numbers and letters—the numbers one through ten and the twenty-two letters of the Hebrew alphabet. Numbers are both physical and abstract; physical because of our ten fingers and toes, and the ability to count real objects, such as sheep in a herd, and abstract because we use numbers to describe complex ideas and laws of nature.

Letters, too, describe reality while remaining apart from it. In ancient Hebrew, as in most other early alphabets, individual letters represented objects. The first letter, Aleph, means "ox," the second letter, Beth, means "a house" (the birthplace of Jesus, Bethlehem, means "house of bread"). And yet, letters are not the objects themselves, they are signs (the Hebrew word for letter, *oht*, also means "sign," or "omen"). With the creation of letters humans took a great leap beyond the physical world into the abstract. Do we wonder that the ancients saw letters as mystical, even eternal? In the Kabbalistic tradition, the Hebrew letters existed before Creation, and God used them to bring the universe into existence.

The two powers, letters and numbers, join together through the placement of letters into groups, three mother letters, seven double, and twelve simple. The Sefer Yetsirah actually declares that all twenty-two letters come from the second sephirah (the first contains the Creator's pure spirit), while the fourth sephirah created the merkavah itself. At the same time we can think of the three mother letters as the three "supernal" sephiroth on the tree, Kether, Hokhmah, and Binah.

Similarly, we can connect the seven double letters to the seven lower sephiroth, Chesed, Gevurah, Tiferet, Netzach, Hod, Yesod, and Malkuth. We might say that the three signify the principles of creation, while the seven bring us to the reality. Over time, the seven lower sephiroth also came to represent the seven "planets" visible to the naked eye (Sun, Moon, Mercury, Venus, Mars, Jupiter, and Saturn), and therefore the seven "heavens" that supposedly surrounded Earth in concentric spheres (Hermann Haindl has followed a modern system of linking the planets to the sephiroth—see chapter five). In another link between the "work of creation" and the "work of the chariot," seven is also the number of the hekhaloth, or palaces, that the mystic must travel in the descent of the merkavah.

As well as mythological sevens, we can see in this vital number such "real" sevens as the colors of the rainbow, the seven chakras (energy centers) of the human body, and the seven notes of the musical scale. In the separation of three and seven that began in the Sefer Yetsirah, seven also came to signify the seven days of Creation described in Genesis. Again, the three higher sephiroth (the mother letters) embody the principles of existence, and the seven lower ones the cosmos that came out of those principles. The fundamental difference between the three and the seven appears on the tree in the abyss between the top three sephiroth and the other seven.

Just as the seven double letters represent the planets and the days of the week, so the twelve simple letters signify the twelve Hebrew months (the Hebrew calendar is lunar, but with periodic adjustments to realign the months with the solar year). And like all twelves, they refer as well to the zodiac, the eternal circle that lies beyond the seven planetary spheres.

The Sefer Yetsirah brought radical new ideas into the mystical tradition. It said that God did not create the universe out of nothing, through simple statements such as "Let there be light." Instead, God created first a structure, the ten sephiroth and the twenty-two letters, and used them to create the physical world. When we first ponder this idea, it might seem to move the Creator far away from us. And yet it gives us the possibility, however difficult, to come to know the divine through knowing the structure. Scientists often speak of the laws of nature this way, that they allow us to approach the truth of existence, even to grasp "the mind of God." Ever since the Sefer Yetsirah, Kabbalists have seen the sephiroth and letters in exactly this way, as a means to approach the unknowable Creator. The brilliance of the tree lies in its perfect combination of the two symbolic forms, the ten sephiroth and the twenty-two letters, in a form that evokes both the ladder and that most ancient and organic of symbols, a tree. Nevertheless, some thousand years would pass before that great image came fully into being.

And before that happened, another very powerful idea would emerge, as central to Kabbalah as the tree itself: the four worlds of Atzilut (emanation), Beriah (creation), Yetsirah (formation), and Assiyah (action). The idea first appeared in print (of course, it may have been much older) in the early twelfth century (1100s), in a work called Masekhoth Atsiluth (Treatise on Emanation) by Jacob Ha-Nazir.

One of the earliest references to a tree comes in Sefer Ha-Bahir (The Book of Brightness) from 1180. There we read, "All the divine powers form a succession of layers and are like a tree." The Bahir also gives us an origin for the word "sephirah." It does not come from "sphere" (a common assumption even today) but from the Hebrew *sappir* for "sapphire."

According to Judith Laura, in her remarkable book *Goddess Spirituality for the Twenty-First Century*, the Bahir greatly developed the symbolic language of the Kabbalah. Where the Sefer Yetsirah treated the sephiroth abstractly, as numbers, the Bahir described them poetically, as divine qualities—vessels, kings, voices, and other aspects. Approximately one hundred years later, the greatest of all Kabbalist works, the Zohar, would develop the sephiroth still further in stories, layers of meaning, and dense symbolism. The Tree of Life takes all these wondrous qualities and mysteries and codes them into that structure, which manages to be both simple and complex at the same time.

The Bahir contributed another important idea, one that has become even more important in modern times, as women claim their place in the study and practice of Kabbalah. This idea is the Shekhinah as the female aspect of God. In the Bible, this term refers to God's "indwelling presence" in the ark. This means that the divine energy physically enters the human world. Mystically, we might say that the presence completed the process of creation (even though it takes place at the time of Moses, thousands of years after the "beginning"). Before the Shekhinah entered the ark, God and God's creation remained separate, like a human fetus before the soul enters it. God talked to Abraham, and intervened in human events, and gave messages to Joseph and others. But we could say that the world truly came alive when the Shekhinah came to dwell in it.

We should point out that we are not speaking literally. The biblical account forms a metaphor, what the Zohar calls a "mystery of mysteries."

We can find similar stories of the divine presence entering the physical world in many other traditions, such as the Celtic/Christian myth of the Holy Grail.

The Bible describes the Shekhinah as a kind of energy. Over time, the term becomes more specific and real—and feminine. The Shekhinah came to mean the spiritual body of Israel, and the soul of humanity. Even in the Bible the mystics have tended to see these things as feminine (like many other Hebrew terms, including Kabbalah and Torah, Shekhinah is grammatically feminine, similar to the Greek word for "soul," *anima*).

In the Bahir, and then more fully in the Zohar, the Shekhinah becomes a female figure, a kind of "Hebrew Goddess" (the title of Raphael Patai's book on the subject). The Zohar describes how the Shekhinah (the female aspect of God) actually left the King (the male aspect) to follow Israel in its exile. We can look at this as a metaphor for all humanity, and say that we all live in exile from the divine—our true selves—and the Shekhinah represents that part of us that never loses the knowledge of who we really are. We could look at the Tree of Life as a way for us to return to full awareness.

Later Kabbalists, especially Isaac Luria, identified the Shekhinah with Malkuth, the final sephirah, usually understood as the material world. It was Luria who taught that Adam saw the beauty of the Shekhinah/ Malkuth and mistook her for the entire tree. This caused the exile from Paradise (PaRDeS). Again, we ourselves make the same mistake over and over with our limited perceptions.

Kabbalah comes from a patriarchal tradition, and one limitation of patriarchy is a tendency to distort and limit the feminine. In some Kabbalist writings, the Shekhinah becomes negative, harsh, even associated with filth (though to be fair, the primary image is of the beautiful bride, the queen). The modern goddess movement has changed our perceptions. Seeing the importance of female representations of the divine, both in prehistoric times and in our own consciousness, has given new balance to Kabbalah. Herman Haindl's art, first in the Tarot and now in the painting of the tree, has always shown his deep understanding of the vital power that comes from the female energy of life.

By general agreement among Kabbalists, the greatest literary work in the tradition is the Zohar, a title that means "splendor" or "radiance." Written around 1280 by Moses de Leon, the book describes itself as written over a thousand years earlier by a great rabbi named Simeon bar Yohai. Supposedly, bar Yohai received the truths of the Zohar as part of a secret oral tradition that went all the way back to Adam in the Garden of Eden. For many centuries people believed this account of the Zohar's composition and considered de Leon simply the publisher.

In the 1930s, when the historian Gershom Scholem demonstrated, through linguistic and other means, that de Leon himself wrote the Zohar, Kabbalists and Orthodox Jews were outraged. Even today, you will find books that insist that Simeon bar Yohai composed the Zohar. However, poet and translator David Rosenberg (in his book *Dreams of Being Eaten Alive: The Literary Core of Kabbalah*) tells us that de Leon worked with a group of people. And after de Leon died, his wife actually confirmed that he wrote the Zohar.

If it was known at the time how the book came into the world, why did people choose to believe the literal text? There is something in us that yearns for authority and absolute truth. The older something is, the more mysterious its origin, the more we can believe it truly comes from divine sources. We want to believe in teachings that are fundamentally different than anything we ourselves, or ordinary mortals, might make up or write on a page. So the Torah must come directly from God on top of a mountain, the Qur'an dictated directly into Mohammed's ear, the Book of Mormon (a modern example) given on golden tablets—and the Zohar written in a cave from knowledge an angel gave to Adam.

This same need pushes us to believe that the Tree of Life is a literal portrayal of the structure of the cosmos. It is, in fact, a brilliant and inspired metaphor developed through successive generations as a way to help us perceive our own relation to the divine forces that have shaped us.

Part of the brilliance of the Zohar lies in its construction. Like the Talmud, it takes the form of rabbis interpreting the Torah together. But instead of straightforward explanations it gives us parables, images, poetry, and myth—along with warnings that we should not take these accounts literally. Thus, we go deeper and deeper into its mysteries.

The impulse to tell mystical tales comes from a very deep place in the human mind. It is not even restricted to those with great training. Here is an example that I include partly because it is fresh in my mind as I write this but mostly because it shows that mystical profundity does not depend on training, or even maturity. An eleven-year-old boy I know, Max Siblo-Landsman, recently told his mother that when the Torah tells us Moses raised his staff and parted the waters so the people could pass to safety, what it really means is that God opened the thighs of the mother so that the children of Israel might be (re)born out of slavery into freedom.

We could spend many pages explicating this vision; if it had appeared in the Zohar (where it would fit right in), people probably would write volumes about it. Now Max, of course, does not believe that an actual mother (we might say Goddess) lay in Egypt pregnant with the Israelites, or that an actual hand came down from heaven to deliver the baby. He understands that the truth of any story about God lies in its meaning. And this is the key to understanding Kabbalah and the tree.

Nevertheless, there is one great difference between Max Siblo-Landsman and Moses de Leon. The stories in the Zohar do not just reflect insight, they come from a long and detailed system of esoteric thought that goes back at least a thousand years before de Leon, to the Sefer Yetsirah. The Zohar takes the concepts, especially of the sephiroth, and builds upon them. For example, it is the Zohar that tells us of the inverted tree: "Now the Tree of Life extends from above downwards, and is the sun which illuminates all" (quoted by Roger Cook in *The Tree of Life*). So much of modern Kabbalah, with all its emphasis on the perfection of the tree, draws its inspiration (if not all its doctrine) from the Zohar. Even some of the names we use come from the Zohar. According to Judith Laura, it was the Zohar that titled the first sephirah Kether (crown), for it originally bore the title Ru'ach (spirit). The Zohar also developed the idea of the En Sof as the source of the emanations.

In 1492 the Christian king and queen of Spain expelled all Jews and Muslims who would not convert to Christianity. Rarely in history can we so pinpoint the end of a glorious five-hundred-year civilization. With the Jews in a new exile, the center of Kabbalistic thinking almost improbably returned to the Holy Land. Specifically, it found a home in a tiny town in the Galilee region (not far from where Jesus taught) called Safed. According to tradition, Simeon bar Yohai himself lies buried in the cemetery on the hillside below the town (in a large tomb painted sky blue).

One of the great Safed thinkers who shaped later visions of the tree was Moses (a popular name for Jewish teachers) Cordovero, who wrote his great work *Pardes Rimmonim* (*The Orchard of Pomegranates*) before his twenty-seventh birthday. This will surprise those who have heard that no one could study Kabbalah before the age of forty. In fact, the other great Safed Kabbalist, Isaac Luria, died at the age of thirty-eight!

Among his other ideas, Cordovero developed further the nature of the En Sof. That statement is actually ironic, for Cordovero stressed that we can know nothing of the En Sof, not even its nothingness. It lies totally beyond us. The En Sof and Kether are not the same, Cordovero taught, a confusion still found among people today. Instead, Kether, like all the sephiroth below it, comes *from* the En Sof.

At the same time, he taught that Kether, like the En Sof, cannot be known directly. Instead, Cordovero proposed that we come to a sense of Kether through Da'ath, that hidden sephirah whose name means "knowledge." He further suggested that three lights shine beyond the tree, though they also could shine through Kether, Hokhmah, and Binah. Centuries later, modern occultists would describe three layers of removal beyond the tree: Ain Soph Aur (boundless light), Ain Soph (boundless, beyond the concept of light), and finally Ain (the void), removed from all concepts entirely (Ain Soph is another way to spell En Sof).

Cordovero was among the first to describe pathways between the sephiroth, including the idea that divine light could travel in several possible directions from a particular sephirah. This doctrine became the twenty-two pathways so vital to our modern concepts of the tree. We also find an interesting reflection in modern physics, with the multiple pathways an electron might take at any possible moment. In yet another influential idea, Cordovero gave colors to the sephiroth. In the Haindl painting we find the colors in the Hebrew name for each sephirah, and through subtle lights that permeate the circle.

Perhaps most important, however, Cordovero developed the doctrine of polarity, still vital to the way we look at the tree today. The sephiroth on the right become representative of the active principle, associated with maleness, light, expansion, and mercy. The sephiroth on the left became an expression of the female principle, with qualities of darkness, passivity, contraction, and justice. The central pillar then becomes the path of harmony.

Once again, Da'ath comes into play, now as the mediator between male Hokhmah (wisdom), or the supernal father, and female Binah (understanding), or the supernal mother. When we know that Da'ath (knowledge) carries qualities of sexuality, we understand that this mediation involves a union on all levels. Remember, too, that Da'ath allows us to know Kether—a knowledge beyond rational investigation.

Why is Da'ath hidden? Partly, of course, it comes from the shape of the tree, with three sephiroth pointing upward and seven pointing downward, with a seeming gap—or abyss—between them. We cannot actually put an extra sephirah at that point, because the Sefer Yetsirah tells us "There are ten sephiroth. Ten, and not nine; ten, and not eleven."

In Kabbalah, however, any such "accident," such as the space between the three and the seven, becomes an invitation to deep meaning. So we come to that idea of the Tree of Knowledge hidden inside the Tree of Life. Through Cordovero, knowledge becomes the power that activates the tree and makes it alive. This is one reason why Da'ath means sexuality, for sexual energy infuses all life. Because Da'ath is hidden, we can say that it does not really occupy that one spot between the three and the seven, but moves through the tree.

In Kabbalist tradition, knowledge is indeed the quality that brings the tree to life, for we come to the vast meanings of the tree through that most Jewish of qualities, study. Nevertheless, Da'ath "hides" because it involves an awareness that most of us cannot reach. Our knowledge concerns ordinary day-to-day existence, the things we learn in school or from our families and friends, the assumptions and prejudices of our society. In a sense, we do not really know anything—in the esoteric sense—of absolute reality unshaped by cultural beliefs.

Partly, Da'ath is secret because the knowledge we call Kabbalah (or Sufism, or Tantra, or Egyptian mysteries, or any of the other names for the paths of truth) is secret. It requires ways of thinking most people do not want to pursue. And it is secret because it recognizes that sexuality and spirituality are the same, the very life of the cosmos.

Following imagery and ideas in the Zohar, Cordovero sexualized the tree. Tiferet became the "son" of Hokhmah and Binah's sexual union, and in turn Tiferet will marry Malkuth, identified both as the Shekhinah and the Sabbath Bride. According to Judith Laura, Chesed and Gevurah aid in arousal through their masculine and feminine qualities. The bottom four sephiroth—the triangle of Hod, Netzach, and Yesod, plus Malkuth—actually become sexual organs. Netzach and Hod form testicles, with Yesod the penis that gives its seed to Malkuth, the vagina of the Shekhinah. Centuries after Cordovero, the occultist Aleister Crowley would suffer condemnation for suggesting that sex magick plays a vital role in the Tree of Life. Coming out of late Victorian times, he may have shocked people, but he was hardly the first to take the tree in that direction.

And yet, as always, we need to avoid too literal or simplistic an interpretation. Just as eleven-year-old Max Siblo-Landsman does not believe an actual hand parted the thighs of an actual mother lying at the shore of the Sea of Reeds, so Moses Cordovero's sex organs on the Tree of Life are metaphors for the flow of energy that makes up existence.

The ancient esoteric doctrine "As above, so below" (see further in this chapter for the origin of this expression) reminds us that we understand divine existence through a close understanding of our own, as long as we do not get stuck in the literal. The message of the union between above and below appears in a different way in Genesis, when the Creator tells the unknown audience, "Let us make man in our image." And indeed, Kabbalists and others, such as the Jains of India, have meditated on the precise dimensions of God's human-shaped body. The point here, however, is not to believe that God has fingers and toes and genitals. Instead, we can understand our own bodies, our own sexuality, as doorways to a deeper truth.

And so it is with Herman Haindl's vivid painting. Does he suggest that a large white bird really flies across Tiferet, or a snake winds around

Hokhmah? Of course not. The images allow Hermann—and us—to perceive the qualities that make the abstract image truly a Tree of Life.

A generation after Cordovero, Isaac Luria occupies a special place in Kabbalah history. His ideas about Creation amount to a new myth, while his spiritual exercises to bring about *yihud* ("union" between the male and female aspects of God), and *tikkun olam* ("heal the world," a restoration of cosmic wholeness) became central to Kabbalist practices. In this way, Luria brought together the contemplative and practical approaches.

According to legend, Luria was a child prodigy, first in Jerusalem where he was born, then in Egypt, where he and his mother went to live with his uncle after his father died. The young Luria became a renowned scholar of traditional Talmudic interpretation. Then one day, at the age of seventeen, he bought a copy of the Zohar from a peddler. Unlike so many who have read the great work and found it beautiful but hard to penetrate, Luria saw below the surface to the wondrous secrets and knew his path in life. He journeyed to Safed, where he quickly commanded a following so devoted that Chaim Vital, his chief disciple (who was actually the one who wrote down Luria's teachings) spoke of him as a human angel. Luria's tomb, in the same Safed cemetery as Simeon bar Yohai, has become a place of pilgrimage. People come there to pray, and to meditate, and even to leave written messages (often for dead relatives) in the cracks in the headstone.

Where Cordovero illuminated doctrine, Luria broke into new territory. One of mysticism's most radical thinkers, he described how the En Sof brought forth the tree. God was everything—all existence—but, being everything, could not know itself. And so the Infinite needed to create something Other. But how could it do this when it filled all existence? And so God contracted. The Hebrew word for this is *tzimtzum.*

Previous Kabbalists had used this term to mean that the divine focused special attention on some aspect of the cosmos. Some modern people, especially women Kabbalists, have compared tzimtzum to birth contractions, as if the female aspect of God labored to give birth to the universe. Luria, however, compared it to a shrinking, like a penis after intercourse. The tzimtzum concentrated the divine into a single unknowable point, with emptiness all around.

Into this emptiness the Creator poured forth the lights that took shape as the sephiroth. If we recall Genesis, we will remember a darkness apparently separate from God, for the spirit of God "hovers" over the face of the waters. And then God proclaims, "Let there be light!"

Luria further developed a concept that has influenced Kabbalah ever since, known as *shiverah*, or "the breaking of the vessels." The term describes a cosmic catastrophe that produced a broken universe. The tree consists of vessels (the sephiroth) made to contain the divine energy. Kether bore the light with ease, but Hokhmah and Binah became strained. And then the next six—Chesed, Gevurah, Tiferet, Netzach, Hod, and Yesod—shattered. The spiritual light rose up and returned to Binah, the supernal Mother, while the physical remains, sometimes called shards or husks (in Hebrew *klippoth*) fell into the physical world. There they became both dense matter and the source of evil.

In a variation of this idea, the En Sof actually created Adam Kadmon, the cosmic human, before the sephiroth and the four worlds. Great lights poured from all the openings in the head of this great being. Some of the lights became letters and sacred names, an idea that gives a mythological structure to the somewhat intellectual insights of the Sefer Yetsirah. Once again, the light entered vessels, the top three held and the next six broke, leaving the final vessel, Malkuth, to receive the broken pieces.

If all this seems remote from what we think of as reality, consider the current scientific doctrine of the Big Bang. Before Creation, all existence lay concentrated in a single primordial point, a so-called "singularity." People often ask what existed outside that point, and the only answer is, "Nothing." And yet it is hard not to picture an emptiness that will receive the universe to come. Further, the scientists say we cannot know anything of the actual nature of this singularity, for it existed before the moment of Creation, and is therefore outside the laws of nature. Does this sound like the En Sof, especially after the tzimtzum, the contraction into an unknowable point?

Something then happened, a random "fluctuation" in the singularity, and energy exploded into the Big Bang. In this first micro-instant no particles or even laws of nature existed—no physical universe as we understand it—only energy. Light, like that which poured from the head of Adam Kadmon. What caused light to become matter? So far, modern cosmologists have not attempted an answer. Perhaps when they do, the description will reflect the Kabbalist myth.

Lurianic doctrine does not leave the cosmos in a helpless, shattered state. Instead, we find tikkun olam, the restoration. On the mythic level the sephiroth change and become faces and characters. Kether becomes the "great face," or "long-faced one," like an old man with a beard. Hokhmah and Binah become Father and Mother, and with the sparks that returned to Binah—"the female waters"—they procreate and produce a son, the "short-faced one," made up of the six shattered vessels.

Malkuth becomes the son's bride, in two forms, named for the two wives of Jacob, Leah and Rachel. On weekdays, Jacob (the short-faced one) takes Leah as his partner, but she only reaches as far as his chest. On Sabbath, Friday night, and Saturday, Rachel comes forth, and she and Jacob make love face-to-face. This opens the way to restoration.

However, tikkun cannot happen by itself. Humans must actively participate. We must focus our energy and actions to the liberation of the light and the reunification of the male King and the female Shekhinah. One way we do this is through a kind of spiritual sex magic. On the Sabbath we make love with our partners, but in a meditative way, so that we go beyond our egos and become channels for the male and female divine as they yearn for yihud (union). Such ideas may shock those who have grown up with the assumption that religion is anti-sexual, or that sex is the enemy of purity. We do not have space here to go into the history of that idea; we will only point out that the esoteric tradition has always recognized the spiritual power of the sexual drive.

Like other Kabbalists, Isaac Luria belonged to a patriarchal culture, and so he designed his yihudim exercises for men to do with their wives. One of the great movements of our time has been the liberation of esoteric possibilities to all people. Thus, lesbians and gay men have shown how sexual and spiritual union does not depend on male and female polarity. Women in general have restored the power and place of the female, not just in the narrow range of sexual magic but in all areas of spiritual truth. In regard to sex, Wiccans invoke the marvelous words of Doreen Valiente, in her poem "The Charge of the Goddess": "All acts of love and pleasure are my rituals."

The Haindl painting restores the tree's physicality on many levels. Its complex imagery revels in all aspects of life. While it does not directly show sexual union, it does give us the sensuality of the world. At the same time it suggests the deeper realms beyond the physical, so that we begin to go beyond the illusion that isolated Adam from Paradise—the belief that the world in front of us is all that exists.

We all share responsibility for the great work of tikkun, for we each must learn to recognize and liberate our own aspect of divine light. Luria taught that this restoration can take many lifetimes, and so he invoked an older Kabbalist idea of reincarnation, called in Hebrew *gilgul*, a word sometimes translated as "transmigration of souls." While it is a mistake to think of Luria as somehow modern (many of his rules and practices would seem almost bizarre to people today), his doctrine of tikkun over many lifetimes does resemble some of today's versions of reincarnation. We do not just learn about our past lives as a source of amusement or self-awareness, we assume that we go into each life in order to learn and to accomplish tasks our souls set for ourselves. Perhaps all these individual lessons and tasks serve an overall goal beyond our individual needs, that of the restoration of the world.

So far we have looked at the Jewish tradition of Kabbalah. Kabbalah is indeed Jewish in its origin and character. Even today, Christian and occult Kabbalists will use Hebrew names for the sephiroth and Hebrew letters for the pathways. The Sefer Yetsirah, Isaac Luria, and other rabbinical sources still inspire us. However, Kabbalah moved into the Christian world relatively early, where it eventually merged with the Western Hermetic tradition (named for Hermes Trismegistus—see below). As early as the beginning of the thirteenth century, Ramon Lull began to introduce Kabbalist ideas to the educated Christian audience.

In the late fifteenth century, some forty years after the first known Tarot cards appeared (in northern Italy), the philosopher Giovanni Pico della Mirandola studied translations of Kabbalist texts and began to make them known to a wider public. The great mystic Jakob Boehme followed, and in the sixteenth century Heinrich Cornelius Agrippa further developed Christian Kabbalah in *De Occulta Philosophia.*

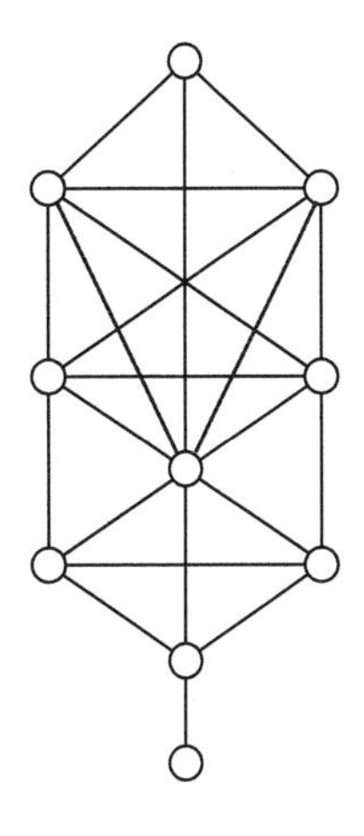

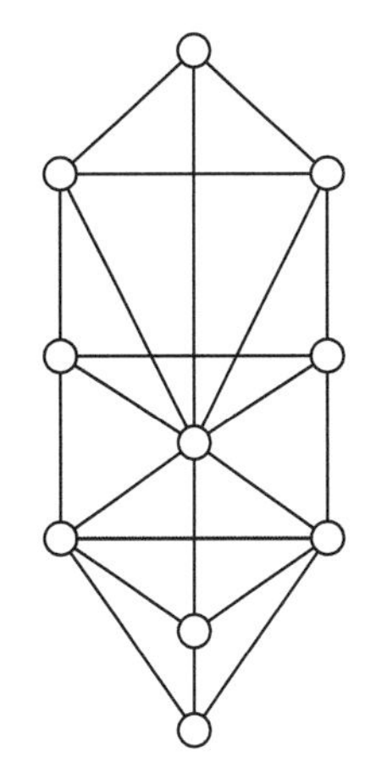

Possibly the most important figure for our study here is the sixteenth-century philosopher Athanasius Kircher. It was Kircher who developed the version of the tree that Western Kabbalah still uses today. Many people interested in Kabbalah do not know that there are several versions of the Tree of Life. They all have the ten sephiroth (plus Da'ath), and they all have the twenty-two connecting lines, but different teachers have connected the lines in different ways. For example, in Isaac Luria's version of the tree (above, left), only one line, from Yesod to Malkuth, connects the bottom sephirah, Malkuth, to the nine above it. In Kircher's Western Kabbalah version (above, right), three lines run into Malkuth, from Netzach and Hod as well as from Yesod. Kircher's version of the Tree is the one used by Hermann Haindl.

The greatest innovation in Christian Kabbalah is—as we might guess—the introduction of Christ onto the tree. Christians identify him with Tiferet, the center where all the lines converge (Hermann Haindl has painted him on the right side, the masculine pillar as well as the pillar of mercy and compassion). For many Christians the crucifixion and resurrection already has restored divine harmony, so that the reunification of polarities becomes less urgent. The tree, then, becomes a means of drawing closer to God, and especially Christ. However, since the Hermetic tradition does work with polarities, especially male and female, the Lurianic tradition still holds.

Mythologically, Christians believe that the cross came from the actual wood of the Tree of Life. In a more symbolic way we can say that Christ himself becomes the tree, or replaces it, for Christians consider Christ the very source of life. And Christians spread the gospel so that knowledge of Christ will make possible the life-giving qualities they find in him. Thus, for Christian believers, knowledge opens up the way to life.

Similarly, Jews implicitly describe the Torah as a replacement for the original tree in the chant when returning the scroll to the ark: "She is a Tree of Life for those who cling to her." Now, since people study the Torah, it acts as a Tree of Knowledge. But that study brings life, for it shows Jews how to understand and follow God's *mitzvoth* (literally "commandments," but with the suggestion of both "blessing" and "opportunity"). And so once again, exoterically as well as esoterically, the Tree of Life lies within the Tree of Knowledge.

Another Christian change concerns the three highest sephiroth. For some Christian Kabbalists these become the Father, Son, and Holy Spirit. Another version, that perhaps stays closer to the earlier visions, would make Kether the Creator (or the Spirit), Hokhmah the Father, and Binah—the supernal mother—Mary. This, of course, places Mary on a divine level with God, something the orthodox churches have always refused to do (it was not until 1950 that the Roman Catholic Church declared that Mary dwelt in heaven, alongside her son).

For the modern esoteric tradition of the tree, the most important innovation comes with an idea the great rabbis (and probably the Christian mystics as well) would have considered very strange, if not downright scandalous. This is the link of Tarot cards with the sephiroth and pathways.

In 1781, a Mason and esoteric researcher named Antoine Court de Gébelin wrote of a personal discovery about the popular card game Les Tarots. De Gébelin was in the course of writing a nine-volume work called *Le Monde Primitif* (*The Primitive World*). In the eighteenth century "primitive" did not mean savage and uncivilized, as it tends to mean today. Instead, it recalled a golden age in which people lived in harmony with divine principles and with knowledge lost to us today.

During his work he chanced to visit a certain Madame la C. de H., who wanted to show him the latest fad, a card game originally played in

Italy, and then southern France. Court de Gébelin wrote how he looked at the cheap, brightly colored cards and was struck with a revelation. The twenty-two trumps—cards not found in ordinary playing decks, containing allegorical images such as "the Pope," "Death," "the Hanged Man," etc.—were in fact a very ancient Egyptian book of secrets, created by the god of magic and wisdom, Thoth, also identified as Hermes Trismegistus. Hermes was the Greek god of magic, while Trismegistus means "thrice-great."

Supposedly, Thoth gave these images to his disciples to initiate them into the mysteries of existence. Knowing, however, that ignorance would replace knowledge as the way of the world, the wise magicians at some point disguised their great lessons as a lowly card game. In this way, they would escape the notice of authorities but still remain in plain view, since the appeal of games and gambling never dies. When an initiated person came across them, he would recognize their true value, and so the "game" would come to life as a book of wisdom.

Court de Gébelin did not directly link the Tarot cards to Kabbalah. He did, however, say that the twenty-two cards represented the twenty-two letters of the "Egyptian alphabet, common to the Hebrews and the Orientals." Egyptian hieroglyphs are indeed an alphabet, but there are not twenty-two of them. However, there are indeed twenty-two Hebrew letters, and as we have seen these do indeed form one of the bases of Kabbalah. In a supplementary article published in *Le Monde Primitif*, a writer named Comte de Mellet laid out a basic system of correspondences between the Tarot cards and the Hebrew alphabet.

Hermes Trismegistus, supposed designer of the Tarot, was the legendary author of the Emerald Tablet, a work as basic to the Western Tradition as the Sefer Yetsirah is to Kabbalah. In Court de Gébelin's time, people believed the Emerald Tablet to be from ancient Egypt (just as they accepted that Simeon bar Yohai composed the Zohar). In fact, it dates from Hellenistic Egypt, about one hundred years after Christ (some two hundred years earlier than the Sefer Yetsirah).

From the Emerald Tablet comes the famous expression "As above, so below." The actual passage runs, "What is below is like what is above, and . . . what is above is like what is below, to perpetuate the miracle of one thing." In other words, the human body and human experience mirror the divine realms of existence, so that a deep knowledge of ourselves will give us a knowledge of God. In more practical terms, we find here the basis of astrology—that our lives, and events around us, mirror the patterns of the stars and planets.

This idea may seem the same as Kabbalah, and certainly many of the Kabbalists were (and are) astrologers. In fact, we can see a radical difference between the classic Kabbalah and the Emerald Tablet. In Kabbalah, an unknowable En Sof generates a series of emanations, each one denser and more distant from the realm of pure spirit. Only the very last, Malkuth, represents what we think of as physical reality. The sephiroth do indeed mirror each other (especially those on the same pillar), and yet we find that sense of distance between the highest above, Kether-Hokhmah-Binah, and the below of Malkuth. By linking the doctrines of Hermes Trismegistus with Kabbalah through the twenty-two trump cards of the Tarot, Antoine Court de Gébelin enlarged our understanding of the tree. The entire tree becomes a reflection of ourselves; our own experiences a reflection of the tree.

Antoine Court de Gébelin and Comte de Mellet began the link of Tarot and Kabbalah. In the mid-nineteenth century, another French occultist, Éliphas Lévi, developed the link into a system. Originally named Alphonse Louis Constant, he took a Hebrew name to signal his devotion to Kabbalist tradition. Aligning the numbers of the Tarot sequence with the order of the letters, he assigned each card to one of the pathways between the sephiroth.

Hermann Haindl follows this tradition in his painting. If you look carefully at the picture you will see a Hebrew letter and the name of a card on the lines or spaces between the sephiroth. These are not, however, the same attributions that Éliphas Lévi worked out all those years ago. The change comes from a group of Kabbalist magicians formed in England in 1888 whose work left a permanent imprint on the beliefs and practices of the Western tradition. The Hermetic Order of the Golden Dawn lasted only some fifteen years, yet in that time managed to construct a vast system, based on the Tree of Life and the Tarot, that brought together astrology, alchemy, Freemasonry, Rosicrucianism, Pagan gods and goddesses, and ritual magic. After the official breakup of the order, other teachers and groups continued their work, some directly in line with Golden Dawn teachings, others with some revisions.

The prominence of the Tree of Life image today owes a great deal to the work of the Golden Dawn and its successors. We might even argue that the revival of Jewish Kabbalah, and its surprise emergence as a popular movement (endorsed by movie stars and complete with books on how to use Kabbalah to advance your career and make more money) comes from the significance the Golden Dawn gave to the Tree of Life. This is ironic, not just because the Jewish tradition tends not to acknowledge the Western versions (after all, the rabbis would hardly endorse replacing Jacob with Christ at Tiferet!), but also because the Golden Dawn operated in complete secrecy.

Those who joined the Golden Dawn in its heyday took solemn vows not to reveal any of the rituals or doctrines. Only after its breakup did some of the more prominent members (and later on, people influenced by the order) begin to publish the information, sometimes with their own revisions. Prominent among these are A. E. Waite, designer of the world's most popular Tarot, the Rider (named for its original publisher); Israel Regardie, the first to publish all the Golden Dawn papers, including the initiations and rituals; Dion Fortune, author of *The Mystical Qabalah*; Paul Foster Case, creator of the Builders of the Adytum (BOTA) correspondence course, still one of the best ways to learn Tarot and Western Kabbalah; and Aleister Crowley, whom many consider one of the geniuses of the Kabbalist tradition.

The Golden Dawn changed Éliphas Lévi's Tarot attributions on the tree in two important ways. First, they switched two of the trump cards. In the classic French Tarot deck (called Tarot de Marseille), Justice is card eight and Strength is eleven. The Golden Dawn placed Strength at eight and Justice at eleven. As a result, they go on different places on the tree.

More significantly, they moved the Fool from next-to-last to first. The Fool presents a special problem for Tarot Kabbalists. Numbered zero, it does not clearly fit in anywhere in the order. The Golden Dawn's approach, to place it before the card numbered one (the Magician), would seem logical. The problem, however, is that the first letter in the Hebrew

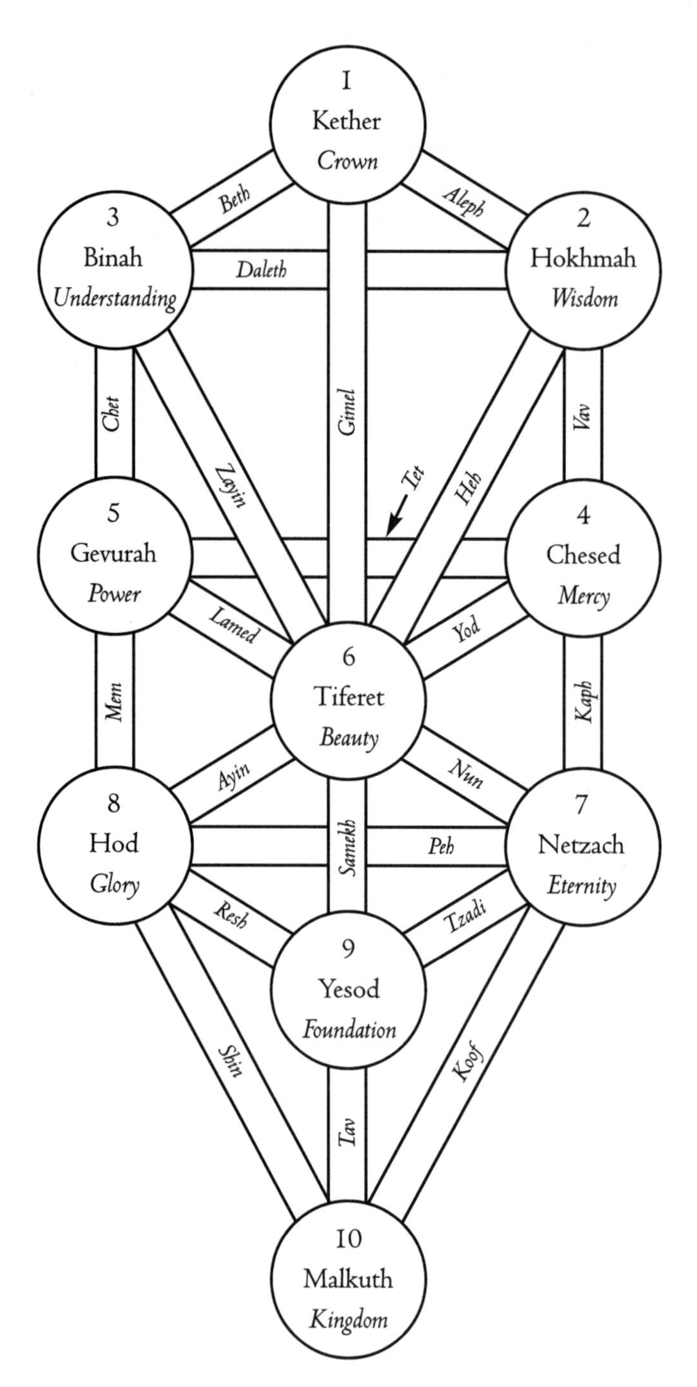

Hebrew Letters on the Tree of Life

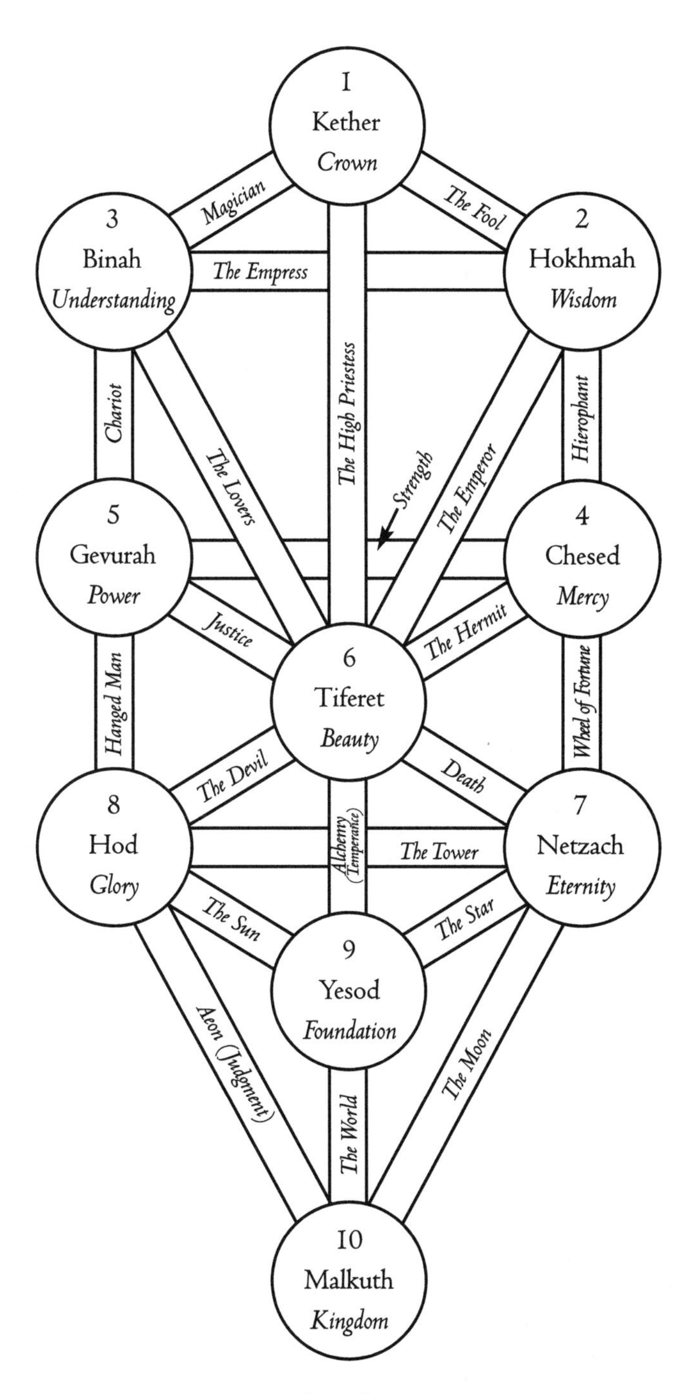

Tarot Cards on the Tree of Life

alphabet does not signify zero, but instead number one. To make the Fool first means that all the cards after it get displaced by one number. That is, card one, the Magician, goes on line two of the tree; card two, the High Priestess, goes on line three, all the way to the last card, the World, numbered twenty-one, which goes on line twenty-two.

This may sound nit-picking, but if you believe that the cards of the Tarot do indeed represent the pathways on the Tree of Life, it becomes clearly important to know which cards go on which pathways. When he created his Tarot deck, Hermann Haindl placed a Hebrew letter on each card, and now that he has painted the tree he has followed the same sequence, that of the Golden Dawn. Thus, we find the Fool, card zero, on the same line as the first Hebrew letter, Aleph, between the first two sephiroth, Kether and Hokhmah.

There are several reasons to follow the Golden Dawn version. First, it is the one most people know, due to the order's great influence on modern Western Kabbalah. Second, most people would agree that the order made good choices, despite the possible confusion of aligning card zero with letter one. The lines on the tree do not just construct a diagram, they signify ideas. Each line carries a meaning by virtue of which two sephiroth it connects. Each Hebrew letter carries a meaning as well—for, as we have seen, the letters symbolize animals or objects that represent allegorical concepts. Finally, the Tarot cards themselves carry complex symbolic ideas. When we look at any line, therefore, we can understand it on at least three levels, and the better those levels support each other, the more we can learn from contemplating them.

In the early twentieth century, when Gershom Scholem began his historical and philosophical study of Kabbalah, the subject lay almost forgotten. Other than small groups of mystical Jews and relatively secretive occult groups, very few people even knew the word, let alone its doctrines and most important symbol. Most likely neither Scholem nor Aleister Crowley would ever have guessed that decades later the Tree of Life would appear on posters or be made into necklaces. The resurgence of Kabbalah at the turn of the century reminds us that truly profound ideas never really die, they just occasionally go into a kind of hibernation, to emerge once again when the culture becomes ready to rediscover them.

FOUR

Four Worlds

The world is very complicated—millions of species, endless ways to get sick, baffling relationships, constant beauty all around us, chaotic weather patterns and natural disasters, and on and on. Something deep inside us insists that so much complication could not just emerge all at once, out of nowhere. In science, we find evolution for the narrow issue of the great variety of species, and the laws of physics and chemistry for the wider picture of the vastness of the universe. In recent years, physicists have observed that the basic forces of existence are so finely balanced that if any of them had been slightly different the universe simply could not exist. This suggests two possibilities; one, that some guiding intelligence shaped these laws, and two, that various "trial" universes existed before this one but collapsed or blew up until this one emerged with just the right balance of forces to sustain itself.

In myth and religion we find variations of both these ideas. Western culture obviously chooses the idea of a Creator God who always knows just what S/He is doing. Other societies have leaned toward the idea of practice makes perfect. In some North and Central American mythologies we find stories of several worlds that existed before this one. While this existence, often the fourth world, has lasted much longer than the others, it still carries many flaws and imperfections. At some distant (or maybe not so distant) time we will emerge into the fifth world, free of all the pain and suffering so common in this one.

If this description sounds alien, consider the European idea of the elements. Fire, water, air, and earth supposedly make up the material world. Those who know the Tarot will know these as the four suits. But a fifth element exists, called ether, linked in Tarot to the twenty-two trump cards found on the pathways of the Tree of Life. The four elements represent physical reality, but ether symbolizes the spiritual. We sometimes call it quintessence, literally the fifth essence, but a word that has come to mean the core truth of something. If we truly could join the four ordinary elements to the quintessence so that spirituality pervaded daily life, it might very well seem as if we had broken through some shell into a new, a fifth, world.

The Sefer Yetsirah comes partly from this sense that the world did not come into being all at once, that we need to look below the biblical account of seven days in which God simply spoke the world into existence. Thus the ten sephiroth emerge as the stages of Creation. And yet this, too, seems too immediate. And so we find the idea of four distinct worlds, each one part of the process, each one further removed from the divine.

Partly this idea comes from the sense that God is somehow far away from us. As we go through our daily lives, with all the demands on us, all the distractions, all the compromises, desires, hopes, disappointments, we do not feel the tangible presence of any divine truth. Our instincts tell us God exists, but is somehow very far away. In Kabbalah this sense takes the form of four distinct worlds, each one with its ten sephiroth of Creation.

The idea of the four worlds also comes from the importance of the number four in Jewish mystical tradition. In the Torah, God's name appears as a word with four letters:

Linguistically, this name seems to be a version of the verb "to be," but not in any actual grammatical form. Tradition describes it as unpronounceable, and therefore a representation of God's ultimate unknowability, the same idea that later became the En Sof.

Jews use a euphemism for God's name, Adonai, a word borrowed from Babylonian that means "Lord." When Christian prayers, or a European translation of the scriptures, include the term "Lord," they actually refer to God's secret and all-powerful name.

Supposedly, in ancient Israel before the fall of the second temple, the High Priest knew the correct pronunciation but could only say it once a year, on the Day of Atonement, in the Holy of Holies at the center of the temple. Even then, he needed to fast and do other purifications before he would dare utter it for, if he could not contain the power it unleashed, he could die. At the very least, his brains might get addled so that he would not be able to find his way out again. Since no one could go in and get him, the other priests would tie a rope around his waist and hold the other end of it as he entered. If he should die or lose his mind, they could pull his body out.

Some readers might recall the Greek myth of Theseus, who entered the labyrinth with a cord tied around him. Ariadne held the other end, and when Theseus had killed the monstrous bull-man, the Minotaur, he could follow the cord back out. The stories are very different, one of sacred power, the other of violence, and yet they share a common image. When we take on a sacred task we leave ordinary human consciousness, and may need some thread to follow so we can return to the outer reality. Similarly, some shamans tell their people to tie their bodies to a pole before they journey to the other world.

The Tree of Life forms both the way into the sacred worlds, and the way back out again. Hermann Haindl's painting in particular shows this double purpose. By including images that are both natural and archaic, everyday and mysterious, and all of it mapped onto the Kabbalist tree, it becomes a kind of roadway for journeys to the different worlds of being.

In European languages, the four-letter name sometimes goes by the term "tetragrammaton," and other times by the four letters Yod-Heh-Vav-Heh (Hebrew reads from right to left, so that the Yod appears on the far right in the calligraphy above). The Western tradition links these to the four elements, fire, water, air, and earth. The elements are on two levels; fire and water seen as more primal, air and earth as more complex, a kind of next generation. At the same time, the elements move rhythmically between male and female—that is, fire and air represent masculine qualities, water and earth feminine. In Genesis God cries, "Let there be light!" and the divine energy (the Big Bang in modern science) penetrates the "darkness on the face of the waters."

We find the same ideas in the Holy Name. Kabbalistic myth describes the Yod and the first Heh as the "father" and "mother," with the Vav and the second Heh as the "son" and "daughter," literally the next generation. And now look at the form of the letters. Both the Yod and the Vav have a kind of phallic shape, while the two Hehs resemble vessels or containers (especially if we turn them upside down). The mother (water) receives the power of the father (fire), and from their union come the daughter (the solid earth) who receives the mind energy of the son (air). To carry this container image further, the space between the vertical line and the bent line forms a kind of spout, to pour out the boundless energy in amounts we humans can accept.

Like the four worlds, the symbolism of both the Name and the four elements follows the stages of Creation from pure energy to the material world. Yod, the smallest letter in Hebrew, symbolizes the first flash of Creation, the instant after the En Sof—or, in modern scientific terms, the singularity—releases the unimaginable energies of the beginning. Water, or the first Heh, signifies the vast emptiness—the deep—that receives this fire and begins to give it form. The Vav extends the Yod in the same way that the creative process—a quality of mind, the element of air—begins to extend the original fiery impulse. Finally, the second Heh, or earth, brings Creation into the solidness of the world we know.

For Western Kabbalists the four elements and the four letters also align with the four suits of the Tarot deck. Wands symbolizes fire, and therefore Yod; Cups is water, the first Heh; Swords is air and Vav; and Stones (or Pentacles or Disks) earth and so the second Heh. The Haindl Tarot further connects these to directions and human civilizations. Wands-fire becomes the east, and India. Cups-water is north, and Europe. Swords-air is south, and Egypt. Stones-earth is west, and North America. In this way, Haindl gives the concepts a more concrete reality, both in nature (the directions, which are not arbitrary but an actual fact of nature created by Earth's axis) and human culture.

The four worlds follow a progression from pure bodiless archetypes to physical "reality." Their names are as follows:

Atzilut, the world of emanation

Beriah, the world of creation

Yetsirah, the world of formation

Assiyah, the world of action

Some writers refer to Atzilut as the world of archetypes. The word here does not mean the figures found in the psychology of Carl Jung. Jung suggested that certain kinds of characters, and perhaps situations, recurred in mythologies all around the world, fairly independent of the local culture. He considered these figures to be "constellations" of energy from the human psyche, and used the old expression "archetypes" to indicate their eternal quality, beyond the individual.

Archetypal for Atzilut means that the sephiroth in this world represent pure principles. We might think of them as similar to Plato's Ideals. The Hebrew word *atzilut* means "proximity," for the idea that this world remains closest to the divine source of Creation. The contemporary Kabbalist Z'ev ben Shimon Halevi says that all laws and dynamics already exist in Atzilut, but nothing can happen because time and space have not come into being. He describes Atzilut as the world of pure divine will.

In order to allow the possibility of change and cosmic evolution, that will requires the other three worlds. Out of Atzilut comes Beriah, the world of creation. Time emerges, and the tree begins to take the form we recognize, for in Beriah light and dark first separate. This separation creates the pillars of justice and mercy, as well as what we think of as natural laws.

According to Halevi, the seven days of the biblical Creation appear here as groups of sephiroth on the tree of Beriah as it literally emerges out of the tree of Atzilut. This may seem confusing, for didn't we say that the seven lower sephiroth, connected to the seven double letters, represent the seven days? We need to remember that Kabbalah is not a simple linear account, an orthodox teaching that we can put into a set of formulae. Many different Kabbalist teachers make up the tradition, and often each one would express a different nuance. Kabbalah, and indeed the tree, become more a way of understanding than a rigid structure.

Thus, we can see the seven days as an aspect of Beriah. Rather than go into all the details of this version (it's somewhat complicated, involving an overlap with Atzilut), we will look at the first and last days. The first day, the separation of light and dark, and therefore the two pillars, becomes the supernal triad of Kether, Hokhmah, and Binah, while the Malkuth of this tree, its bottom sephirah, becomes the place where God rests on the seventh day. In Genesis God proclaims the cosmos as "very good." This expression does not just mean that the Creator approves of his/her handiwork. It implies that the two pillars, justice and mercy, have come into correct balance. Malkuth, after all, lies at the bottom of the middle pillar, harmony.

In Atzilut we saw the emanations of pure will, similar to Platonic ideals. In Beriah we get the completed forms, so that the biblical story tells of God creating each aspect of Creation, including the creatures. But these are still basic types, as if God creates A Lion, A Sheep, A Rose, and finally A Man and A Woman. The next world, Yetsirah, or formation, will allow all the different variations of Sheep, Rose, and Human to begin to emerge.

We saw earlier how the second chapter of Genesis, the one with the Garden of Eden and its two trees, seems to give a different account of Creation from the first. Among other things, the "male and female" of chapter one become Adam and Eve in chapter two. The Kabbalists deal with this paradox by suggesting that a new world and a new tree have come forth, and existence has become more detailed and complex.

In the tree of Yetsirah (the same name as the earliest Kabbalist text), the ideal beings created in Beriah now develop into an endless variety of forms. Here Adam and Eve go through their drama with the snake, the fruit, and the Tree of Knowledge of Good and Evil. Halevi calls this the world of "ever-changing phenomena, as it is worked on by the dynamics of Creation and Divine Will above." Creation and divine will, of course, refer to the two previous worlds (moving backwards, from two to one), Beriah and Atzilut.

The fourth world, Assiyah, is the world of "action," where we ourselves live, the descendants of Adam and Eve after they lost Paradise. The Bible tells us that a river flowed out of Eden to become four famous rivers of the ancient Middle East. Some Kabbalists see these four rivers as the echo of the four worlds—that is, they all flow into Assiyah, but we can see in them the mirror of the previous worlds.

We can visualize the four worlds in relation to the tree in several ways. We can think of four trees side by side, or one below the other, each with ten sephiroth so that the total becomes forty. This is one reason the number forty appears so frequently in biblical stories. In Genesis, God makes it rain for forty days and forty nights to flood the world. The Israelites wander for forty years in the desert. These two stories, flood and desert, emphasize the idea of separation and hardship, just as the idea of four distinct trees breaks up the sense of divine unity. It reminds us of how far we have separated from the Creator. After all, we do not just live in Assiyah, we live in the Malkuth of Assiyah, the very bottom of the final tree.

However, we also can see the number forty as our way to return to a greater consciousness. Moses prepares himself for forty days and nights before he ascends to Mt. Sinai to receive the Torah. He then remains on Sinai for another forty days and nights.

Human beings each have ten fingers and ten toes. When two people make love they entwine their bodies to produce forty extensions of themselves into the universe. We can think of these forty fingers and toes as the sephiroth, no longer separate but blended together. Once again, sexual union becomes the embodiment of spiritual union. The lovers become the four worlds in dynamic movement.

Most Kabbalists do not actually envision four distinct trees standing apart from each other. Instead, they show the bottom half of one tree becoming the top half of the next. The lower tree begins in Tiferet of the higher. In other words, Tiferet, Netzach, and Hod of Atzilut become the Kether, Hokhmah, and Binah of Beriah. The Yesod of the higher tree actually becomes the Da'ath of the lower, and so we might say that it becomes invisible, since Da'ath is the hidden, or invisible, sephirah—or conversely, that Yesod, imagination, makes Da'ath visible. Imagination leads the way to knowledge.

The Malkuth of the higher tree becomes the Tiferet of the lower. However, since the Tiferet of the lower tree becomes the new Kether of the tree below that, a single sephirah actually serves three different functions in three different trees. For example, the Malkuth of the first tree, Atzilut, is the Tiferet of the second, Beriah, and also the Kether of the third tree, Yetsirah. Similarly, the Malkuth of Beriah is the Tiferet of Yetsirah, but also the Kether of the final tree, Assiyah.

If all this sounds confusing, a picture will make it clearer. Here is how the diagram looks for two trees (on the left), and now here it is for all four (right):

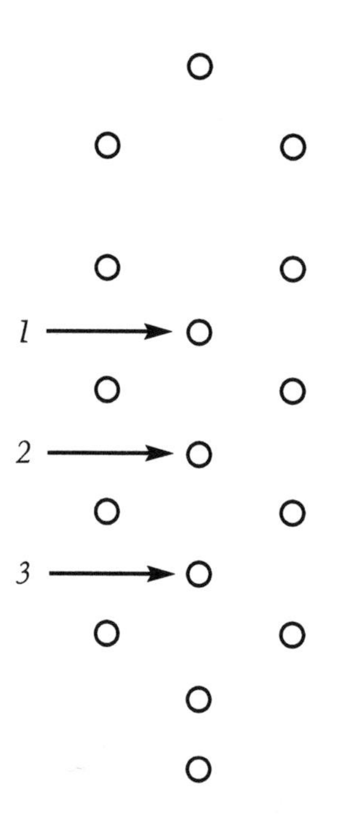

1 *Tiferet of Tree 1, Kether of Tree 2*
2 *Yesod of Tree 1, Da'ath of Tree 2*
3 *Malkuth of Tree 1, Tiferet of Tree 2*

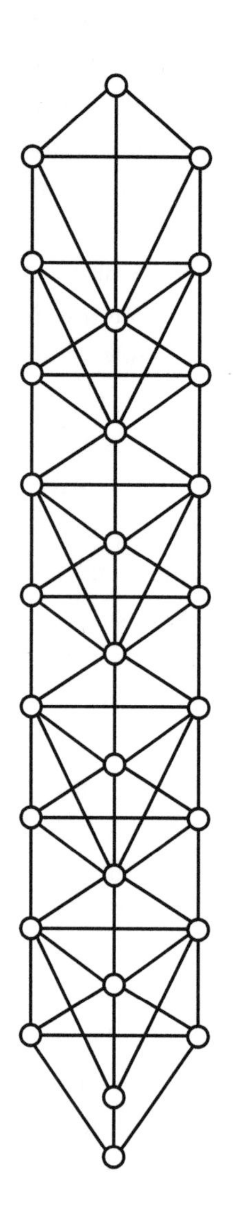

This fully extended diagram is the one most often called Jacob's ladder, simply because it so clearly resembles a ladder-like structure. When the trees overlap this way, the number of distinct sephiroth reduces from forty to twenty-eight. An interesting effect happens, however, for the middle pillar actually becomes ten sephiroth, so we might say that all qualities come to rest in the pillar of harmony. Theoretically, if the meditative journeyer can fully visualize such a large and complex diagram, she or he could climb straight up the middle from Malkuth to Kether.

So far, we have looked at how to extend the single tree into four worlds, either as four separate trees or as one giant overlapping tree. We also can visualize it the other way—that is, all four worlds contained in one tree of ten sephiroth. Here we find Atzilut in the top three sephiroth, Beriah in the middle three, Yetsirah in the bottom three, with Malkuth alone as the representation of Assiyah.

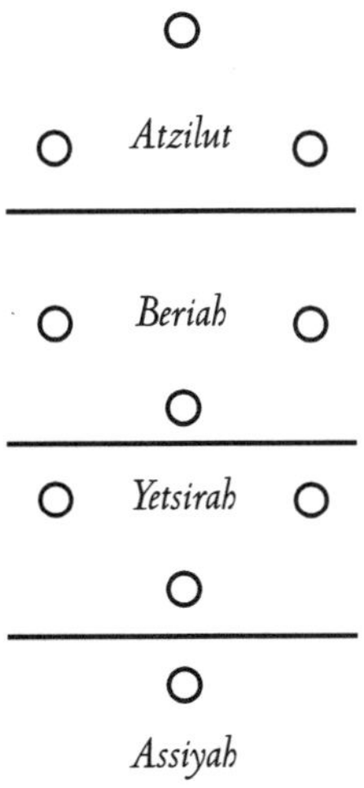

Atzilut	Yod	S	Wands Fire	Chai (Life Force)
Beriah	Heh	D	Cups Water	Neshamah (Spirit)
Yetsirah	Vav	R	Swords Air	Ruach (Intellect)
Assiyah	Heh	P	Stones (Pentacles) Earth	Nefesh (Animal)

When we look at the four worlds in this way, all sorts of correspondences become simplified. Here are a few, starting with the world we experience most directly, Assiyah, and moving upwards to Atzilut.

Assiyah, or action, represents the material world. We find it in the final sephirah, Malkuth (remember Adam's great mistake, that we ourselves repeat, to look at Malkuth—Assiyah—and consider it all of existence). We find it in the final letter of God's name, Heh, for remember, we need to work our way back to divine consciousness. At the same time, we connect it to the P, or peshat, of PaRDeS (Paradise). This is the letter of literal understanding. (With Yod-Heh-Vav-Heh we travel back to divine awareness, while with PRDS, we move forward to put full understanding together, as if we can reassemble Paradise.) Assiyah expresses the element earth and the Tarot suit of Stones (or Pentacles, or Disks, or Coins, according to the deck). Some also connect it to the "animal soul," nefesh, which we might think of as our basic instinct.

Next we come to Yetsirah, the world of formation, found in the triangle of Netzach, Hod, and Yesod. Yetsirah expresses the element air, connected to the third letter in God's name, the stretched-out line of Vav. It also expresses itself in the R, remez, of PaRDeS, the letter of intellectual understanding. Intellect is also the quality of air and the Tarot suit of Swords. The soul level here is Ruach, also seen as the power of intellect.

From Yetsirah we move up to Beriah, the world of creation, expressed in the central triangle of Chesed, Gevurah, and Tiferet. This is the element of water as well as the second letter in God's name (the same as the fourth letter). We find it in the D, or drash, of PaRDeS, the letter of allegorical truth and greater understanding (compared to the narrower intellectual approach of remez). The Tarot suit here is Cups. The deepest quality of the element water is divine intuition; in other words, the ability to get a sense of divine consciousness beyond our limited intellectual grasp. The soul name for this quality is neshamah.

Finally, we ascend from Beriah to Atzilut, the archetypal world of emanation. This world expresses itself in the top triangle on the tree, Kether, Hokhmah, and Binah. Western Kabbalah (most of these correspondences actually come from the Golden Dawn tradition) links this world to the element of fire—pure energy—and the Tarot suit of Wands (or Staves). Atzilut is the first letter of God's name, the short, intense Yod. We also find it in the S, or sod, of PaRDeS, the letter of full mystical understanding. The soul level here is *chai*, which simply means "life," for this is the pure life force beyond the individual three-level soul.

These qualities and correspondences all come from the different Kabbalist traditions (I have tried to put together a unified sense of the structure from both the Jewish and Western Kabbalah). But what happens if we look at the four worlds on the Haindl painting?

The first thing we notice is that there is no obvious separation or borders between the different levels. We do not find abstraction at the top of the tree and conventional realism at the bottom. Instead, we find that the various qualities, from vague shapes and eroded stone to very realistic images, appear all through. This reminds us once more that the powers on the tree do not really keep so strictly apart from each other as the descriptions seem to suggest. Instead, we remember that the tree is a whole, and all its qualities penetrate each other.

And yet we can see subtle qualities in the various levels. The more realistic images tend to show up in the middle sections, while the top and bottom show the eroded archaic qualities so characteristic of Haindl's work. This may seem surprising when we think of the doctrine that the worlds become denser and less pure as they move from Atzilut to Assiyah. But think again of the word PRDS, and that idea that the P and the S, the literal and the mystical, contain the deepest mysteries and the greatest truths. The P and the S correspond to Assiyah and Atzilut.

The Haindl painting actually begins above the tree, with a suggestion of the En Sof. In the center the dark horn tip of the bull in Kether penetrates what seems to be abstract nuances of light. This is consciousness reaching into the world beyond knowing.

On the sides, however, we do get suggestions of images. A kindly face, who resembles Albert Einstein, appears in the upper left. Like a modern Kabbalist sage, Einstein sought to understand the deepest truths in existence, to go beyond the physical phenomena to the underlying reality. A famous story tells of the moment when an eclipse of the sun finally gave a chance to prove the predictions of Einstein's Theory of Relativity. The theory is that physical mass bends space around it. A great mass, like the sun, would bend space enough so that light from other stars would seem to curve as it traveled past the sun. Because we normally cannot see starlight near the sun there was no way to test this suggestion until a total eclipse came. When it did, and the light bent at just the degree that the theory suggested, the whole world celebrated—but Einstein himself seemed almost indifferent. He'd known what would happen. (For more on Einstein, and the possible conjunction between Gnosticism and the Theory of Relativity, see my book *The Forest of Souls.*)

The image of the old man also reminds us of the Kabbalist expression "the Ancient of Days." The phrase first appears in the book of Daniel as a description of God. For some Kabbalists it can mean the original human, called Adam Kadmon, or the Great Face that indeed looks down from the Atzilut triangle of Kether-Hokhmah-Binah.

Next to and slightly below the old man we see crisscrossing lines of varied colors. This is possibly the most abstract formal image in the painting. It suggests those perfect laws of existence associated with Atzilut. On the other side of the tree we see that hint of Christ on the cross, with his crown of thorns. For Christians, the crucifixion represents the moment when the divine eternal entered human history. We might describe this as Atzilut descending into Assiyah.

In the actual triangle of Atzilut—Kether-Hokhmah-Binah—we find images that are old and stonelike. Figures from Hokhmah and Binah seem to yearn for each other. From Hokhmah angelic stone faces move towards the left, while from Binah the delightful image of a flying rabbi stretches his arms to the right. He emerges from a goddess figure who stands up out of Binah, the supernal mother. Outside the actual sephirah of Binah a dark face emerges from the stonelike column. This is the oldest world, where divine will begins to set everything in motion.

When we move down to Beriah—Chesed-Gevurah-Tiferet—the figures become more sharply defined, and yet still with an ancient feel. Here we see the ouroboros-like snake of Chesed, life-giving, eternal, matched by the seeming nest of vipers around Gevurah. The images fit the tension between the two, for they are the epitome of expansion and contraction, mercy and justice. This is Beriah, where the opposites first establish themselves. Tiferet, the very center of the tree and the representation of the heart, resolves the tension by transforming the energy. Instead of snakes, we see a white bird flying toward us.

The white bird becomes still further defined as we move from Beriah, the world of creation, to Yetsirah, the world of formation. Here, in the triangle of Netzach-Hod-Yesod, we see a long-necked swan fly from the right toward a smiling face whose eyes are covered by white wings.

At the bottom triangle, a young lamb looks upwards, as if toward the horned bull in Kether. Just before all the worlds pour into Malkuth, the sephirah of foundation, Yesod, yearns to reunite with its "parent," Kether, far above it.

The world of Assiyah expresses itself in the single sephirah, Malkuth. Instead of a sharply defined, conventional reality we see the return to mystery, with human and animal faces jumbled together on the side, and the sephirah itself as simply a partial disk, with a rainbow halo. We do not see the whole circle here, as we do with the other nine sephiroth. Nature is unfinished, as much a mystery as what lies beyond Kether.

This world of Assiyah all rests on a dark sea, as if in the moment of completion the tree reminds us that at the very beginning of Creation—even before the declaration "Let there be light!" there was simply "darkness on the face of the waters." Looked at as the four worlds, the painting suggests that the two middle sections represent the mind, which sees everything in clear terms. When we move to the physical realm of Malkuth all becomes dark, ancient, and merged together.

A traditional Kabbalist might see this as the "denseness" of the physical world hiding the pure light of the spiritual worlds above it. I think, however, that we can read this another way. If we genuinely look at nature, without the intellectual filters of scientific or cultural concepts, every object, every tree or bird or surge of water, becomes an opening to the wonders of existence.

When we experience the mysteries of Assiyah the worlds become a circle as much as a ladder. The essential quality of Kether, at the top of Atzilut, is undifferentiated energy, the ability to contain everything. Malkuth, too, contains everything, all the marvels of physical creation. That desire of the young animal in Yesod to reunite with its parent in Kether becomes fulfilled in Malkuth. Like the snake biting its own tail around Chesed, the top and bottom sephiroth seem somehow to touch each other, so that the four worlds become a circle, as well as a tree, of life.

We can look at the four worlds on the tree in still another important way, as a map of the human body. As we have seen, the principle of "As above, so below," along with the biblical "Let us make man in our image," teaches us that the shape and functions of the human reflect the divine. We can see this most clearly if we first look at the body and the four letter name of God, Yod-Heh-Vav-Heh. Arrange the letters vertically (with the third letter, the Vav, inside the second) and they take on something of the shape of a human.

Here the Yod becomes the head (we can visualize it in profile, or with a face contained inside the shape). The first Heh forms the shoulders and arms, the Vav the trunk of the body, and the second Heh the pelvic girdle and legs.

Now transfer this to the four worlds. Our feet stand in Assiyah, the physical world. Assiyah means action, and with our legs we move about in this realm of events.

From Assiyah we move up to find our trunks in Yetsirah, the world of formation. Our internal organs dwell here, and each one teaches a lesson. The heart is the seat of emotional truth. Through its beats we understand the basic rhythms of life. The lungs allow us to take in oxygen, the gift from the plants, and to give them back carbon dioxide in return. This exchange teaches us that we do not exist in isolation from other creatures and the world around us. Similarly, the digestive organs remind us that we can only survive through the sacrifice of other living organisms.

Moving upwards again, we discover Beriah, the world of creation, in the first Heh, which forms the shoulders and arms. With our arms and hands, and our ten fingers to remind us of the sephiroth, we reach beyond our own bodies to something greater. Our hands allow us to create, whether it be buildings or art or any of the other wondrous aspects of human civilization. The pure ideas come from the brain, but without arms and hands we could create nothing. And when we do use our Beriatic hands to give shape to our ideas, we do not just make whatever it is we have seen in our minds. New aspects come to light with the physical creation. We learn constantly whenever we make something.

The Yod becomes the head, and the world of Atzilut. The holy fire of pure thought, of ideas and principles, the flash of imagination and insight—these are the qualities that connect us to the divine.

Now transfer these world connections to the tree. Our feet and legs stand in Malkuth, we find the trunks and organs of our bodies in the triangle of Netzach-Hod-Yesod, our shoulders and arms in Chesed-Gevurah-Tiferet, and our heads in Kether-Hokhmah-Binah.

This is one interpretation of the body and the tree, set in terms of the four worlds and the four letters of God's name. When we go through the tree in detail we will see that we can find the body in the ten distinct sephiroth (for example, Tiferet specifically represents the heart).

None of this suggests that the body is in some way divided up, or in distinct sections, or literally separated into different worlds. The real lesson becomes the opposite. Because the body is a single organism, and all its aspects function together, so we learn to see the cosmos of the four worlds, and the Tree of Life, as a single being. As below, so above—from our own bodies, and our own experiences, we learn the nature of the divine.

Before we leave the four worlds we need to look at how these very large concepts can actually work in our lives. In their attempts to comprehend God and Creation, the great Kabbalist teachers often raised their thinking to lofty heights. As important as this work is, we also need to connect it to more immediate self-knowledge and our own struggles to create a meaningful existence.

One way we can do this is through the Tarot. We have already seen how we can link the Tarot cards, with their extensive symbolism, to the four elements, and therefore the four worlds. Remember, too, that we find the twenty-two Tarot trumps on the twenty-two pathways connecting the ten sephiroth. When we put together the abstract ideas of the tree and the worlds with the more concrete images of the cards, we gain a way to grasp the Kabbalah tradition and make it clearer.

But we can do something else with the cards. We can lay them out in readings. We can ask a series of questions based on the spiritual ideas, mix the cards, turn them over one by one, a card for each question, and so find insight into our own specific issues around those very large teachings. When we have gone through the sephiroth in detail, and examined the traditional connections between them, we will look at what it can mean to use the sephiroth as questions in a Tarot reading. We can do the same, however, with the four worlds.

In order to use the worlds as the positions in a reading we first need to see how the overall concepts can apply to people's lives. I discussed the worlds with a monthly class I teach in New York City; here are some of the ideas that emerged.

Atzilut in people's lives connects them to the pure essence of their being. It brings them back to the source of who they are, their own ultimate beginning. If they can touch their own Atzilut, they can see how everything in life is connected, how everything points back to an inner truth. One person described it as like a hologram. In a hologram picture, any piece of the whole contains the entire image. In Atzilut we begin to see how all the seeming fragments of our experience reveal that essential nature. Just as the visionary poet/artist William Blake could see the universe in a grain of sand, so in our moments of Atzilut clarity we can see who we are really meant to be from any moment.

Beriah brings us to the unconscious. I do not mean here the Freudian idea of hidden desires or experiences, but rather a personal connection to the life force. One person in our group called this connection "the soup." Another reminded us that our world is three-quarters water, and our bodies even more so. Remember that in the system we have followed (there are others) Beriah belongs to the element of water. Beriah therefore activates our intuition, and our mythic understanding of truths that we cannot put into words.

At the same time, Beriah is the world where principles begin to separate out of the pure essence of Atzilut. We might think of islands and continents emerging out of the original ocean that covered all of earth. For individual people, Beriah can signify the big ideas that govern their lives. These can include broad ethical principles.

Yetsirah represents the conscious mind. What seemed large and dreamlike in Beriah now takes on the hard edge of reality. This includes our belief systems, made up partly of the cultural ideas we learned from our parents and society, and partly our own truth and experience. The large concepts of Beriah become more detailed, more thought out. Yetsirah also shows us how we see ourselves, our conscious self-image.

In Yetsirah we see the complexity of our lives. We look at past events and plan for the future. We also consider the ethical choices we have made out of those broad principles in Beriah.

In Assiyah we see our actions. The ideas and beliefs of Yetsirah get tested in the reality of events and practical responsibilities. We deal with our bodies and our physical needs, with aging, and loss, and the birth of new things. We struggle with life and the consequences of all the choices we make, both ethically and practically. In Assiyah we get caught up in daily life and can lose the wider vision of the other worlds. At the same time, we feel most deeply alive.

Out of these descriptions we get to ask questions. The reading spread is very simple, the same two questions for each world (for the mechanics of how to do a reading, see the appendix): "Who am I in this world?" and "What is my task in this world?"

Pattern for Readings

Atzilut	1	2
Beriah	3	4
Yetsirah	5	6
Assiyah	7	8

As a sample, here is a brief description of the reading I did for myself.

Who am I in Atzilut? The Sun. In this world of pure essence I experience simplicity and light. I join with basic, unending energy. *What is my task in Atzilut? The Ace of Stones.* I need to bring that perfect light into the material world of day-to-day life.

Who am I in Beriah? The High Priestess. This card fits perfectly, for the High Priestess is the figure who dwells within that "great soup" of myth and dreams and spiritual principles. *What is my task? The Six of Stones.* Once again, the issue becomes to somehow take these very big ideas and make them real. Hermann Haindl gives the Six of Stones the title of "Success." He does not mean monetary success so much as the link of spiritual values and material reality.

Who am I in Yetsirah? The Star. This is a card of renewal. The image on the card goes back to a very primitive state, a world of just rock and water. And yet, compared to the High Priestess, she does not stay in the soup but emerges onto land—in other words, out of intuition into consciousness. The woman bends low and pours water on her head, as if to cleanse herself and start over. In the mental world I renew myself and begin fresh. My task here is *The Universe.* The two together recall Isaac Luria's famous description of the spiritual task that faces each one of us, tikkun olam, or heal the world. As much as I can, I need to use my ideas and abilities to help others.

Who am I in Assiyah? The Five of Wands. Notice that in the three "higher" worlds we saw a trump, or Major Arcana, card for the "Who am I?" question. It fits that in the day-to-day world of Assiyah I would get a pip, or Minor Arcana, card. Hermann Haindl calls this card "Creative Argument." It suggests intellectual engagement and stimulation. In my work I have often tested my own ideas against the wiser sages and teachers who have gone before me. My task here is *The Fool,* the very first card of the Major Arcana. Just as I needed to bring the light of Atzilut Sun into the material world of the Ace of Stones, so here, in the world of action, I need to bring those ideas and arguments back to the spiritual. Just as with Hermann Haindl's painting, Atzilut and Assiyah become linked into a cycle.

FIVE

Tree Overall

By now we have seen how complex Kabbalist ideas can be. Despite the various worlds, and letters, and correspondences, the fullest meaning of the tree emerges when we ponder the sephiroth and their relationships. We have already looked at various qualities of the sephiroth within the context of other ideas about the tree, but now we will go through them more systematically, with special attention to the powerful images in Hermann Haindl's painting.

Before the symbolism of the individual places on the tree we need to consider—once again—some correspondences. In chapter three we looked at the historical development of the many attributions, including such things as color, the seven days of Creation, etc. Readers will have noticed how different teachers developed slightly different systems. Hermann Haindl has followed a modern version, based on the Golden Dawn, with advice from his friend, esotericist Gunther Cherubini. Look at the painting and you will see the following colors suffuse the sephiroth:

Kether—White

Hokhmah—Gray

Binah—Black

Chesed—Blue

Gevurah—Red

Tiferet—Yellow

Netzach—Green

Hod—Orange

Yesod—Violet

Malkuth—Gold

Haindl's astrological attributions for the planets also follow a modern design, one that takes into account the discovery of the three outer planets, Neptune, Uranus, and Pluto. It also includes Earth. In traditional astrology, Earth is the center of the planetary spheres, the focal point of all the influences. The seven "planets"—sun, moon, Mercury, Venus, Mars, Jupiter, and Saturn—all move through the earthly sky. However, Malkuth signifies the physical world, the realm of our daily lives, so that it makes sense to see Malkuth as Earth.

Here are the attributions from Haindl and Cherubini:

Kether—Pluto

Hokhmah—Neptune

Binah—Saturn

Chesed—Jupiter

Gevurah—Mars

Tiferet—Sun

Netzach—Venus

Hod—Mercury

Yesod—Moon

Malkuth—Earth

Notice that the inclusion of Earth for Malkuth leaves no sephirah for Uranus (in a sense, we skip over it as we go from Hokhmah—Neptune to Kether—Pluto). We might, however, consider Uranus as the "hidden" sephirah of knowledge, Da'ath. One quality of Uranus is transformational thought, something we could easily attribute to Da'ath.

We saw earlier how we might find Adam Kadmon—and therefore all humans—in the four worlds. We also can map the human body onto the individual tree through the ten sephiroth (as opposed to the three triangles and Malkuth that we looked at above). As with so much else, different versions exist. Here is one from Charles Poncé in his book *Kabbalah*, a contemporary work that brings together both the ancient Jewish and modern Western traditions. It bases the correspondences on the functions as well as the place in the body.

Kether, the crown, forms the head.

Hokhmah, wisdom, resides in the brain.

Binah, understanding, rests in the heart. Poncé points out that many people, especially in esoteric traditions, have considered the heart the true organ of thinking. The brain governs rational judgment, but the heart gives us the understanding described in the sephirah. Some yoga teachings tell us that the kundalini energy rises up the spine to the brain (Hokhmah), seems to open up the top of the head (Kether), and then moves back down to rest in the heart.

Chesed, mercy, lies in the right arm and hand. For right-handed people, the right arm reaches out to help others.

Gevurah, power, lies in the left arm and hand. In contrast to the right, the left arm can mark a boundary. If we give with the right hand, we hold back with the left. We will see, when we look closely at this sephirah, that we should not think of this as "evil" or negative but as a very necessary quality, for if we give ourselves away we end up with nothing.

Tiferet marks the chest. This is where the Binah heart energy comes to reside (thus joining the upper triangle to the middle). It also forms the site of the lungs, the organ that allows us to exchange energy with the world around us. We breathe in oxygen created by the plants (as a byproduct of photosynthesis) and breathe out the carbon dioxide plants need to live. Breath also forms our connection to the divine. We speak of the breath of life, and in fact such words as spirit, or the Hebrew words *ruach* (spirit), or *neshamah* (soul), literally mean "breath." Kabbalists often describe the four-letter name of God, Yod-Heh-Vav-Heh, as the sound of a breath.

Netzach, eternity, is the right leg. Netzach is an active power, and for right-handed people (the majority) the right leg steps toward our spiritual encounters and victories.

Hod, glory, is the left leg. We might think of glory as the place where we stand, firmly rooted.

Yesod, foundation, represents the genitals, both male and female, for remember that Adam Kadmon signifies the perfect hermaphrodite before separation into male and female.

Malkuth, or kingdom, receives all the energy of the sephiroth above it, and so Poncé comments that Malkuth symbolizes "Adam Kadmon's harmony or completeness" (Poncé, p. 137). We also might think of Malkuth as the base of the spine, the root chakra, and the resting place of kundalini.

Poncé further points out that Kabbalists traditionally depict Adam Kadmon as seen from behind. This imagery stems from the famous passage in Exodus where Moses asks to see God but can only view the Creator from behind, for no one can see God directly and live. The image of Adam Kadmon from behind also has a practical meditative value. Our own bodies will align with the figure, whose right and left sides will match our right and left sides. This way, the heart and other organs will be in the same place as our own. We can visualize Adam Kadmon and then imagine ourselves stepping into the image.

The correspondences allow us to look at the tree as a system. To really make use of the system, however, we need to understand the individual places.

We will begin, again, where the story begins, outside the actual tree, in the unknowable realm of the En Sof. The Haindl painting suggests this mystery by having the top seem to dissolve into a blankness that looks like ancient eroded stone. The idea of the En Sof represents an attempt to penetrate further and further back into the origins of existence. Picture the great mystics deep in meditation. Slowly they follow the path of the tree, from the physical "reality" of Malkuth, step by step, through the levels, until it even becomes possible to cross the abyss of knowledge, even to trace their way back to Kether. But what lies beyond? Where does Kether come from?

Think of the question every child asks when first exposed to religious ideas. "If God created the universe, who created God?" And the parent answers, "Nobody created God. God always existed."

The child pushes on. "But how? Did God come out of nowhere?" to which the parent can only answer, "I don't know, dear. Nobody knows."

By definition, the En Sof exists beyond all our definitions. If you have meditated over a long period you will know that we can let go of all our somethings and perceive the quality of nothing. But this does not mean we have found the En Sof, for this nothing is still a human perception.

The Golden Dawn created the three levels of En Sof as an attempt to push back the boundaries even further. And so beyond Kether lies Ain Soph Aur (the Golden Dawn spelling), the limitless light. It is actually this light that contracts, in the tzimtzum, to that singularity that opens up the Big Bang of Creation. The light itself, however, comes from that greater infinite mystery of the Ain Soph. And we can go even a step further back, to the Ain, the simple void.

The concept of the En Sof has influenced modern mathematics. When Georg Cantor developed his levels of infinity, he used the Hebrew letter Aleph as their sign. Aleph is the first letter in the Hebrew word *en*. Remember, too, that Aleph makes no sound, but only represents the mouth opening before speech, a perfect evocation of the void as it moves to cross the boundary into existence, the something—sound—that will come out of the nothing—Aleph.

Aleph also begins other words in Hebrew, in particular *ani*, or "I." The mystery of self also begins in silence. Like the universe, we originate in a nothingness our egos can hardly contemplate. We, too, are not all the somethings we use to describe ourselves. This is what it really means to say that God created humans in God's image. A blessing in the Reconstructionist Jewish prayer book expresses this idea with succinct beauty. "Blessed are you, the Imageless, who has created me in your image." As above, so below.

Did the En Sof create the sephiroth and the tree as something outside of itself? In other words, is the universe really separate and distinct from its Creator? Kabbalah suggests the opposite, for it teaches that the entire pattern of the sephiroth, and therefore all reality, existed within the En Sof before the beginning. Everything that we see, and everything that we ponder, and everything that we cannot see—it all comes from the divine. And yet—the paradox of Kabbalah and the tree—it still needed to come into being in order to realize itself. We might think of a painter who conceives a magnificent image, down to the last detail. It exists within the painter's mind but she still must bring it alive on the canvas.

Out of En Sof comes the tree. It moves in stages, from Kether down to Malkuth, but so quickly it would seem instantaneous if we somehow could witness it. Kabbalists compare this movement to lightning. Lightning comes from the movement of electricity in the sky, but because the energy travels so quickly we see the entire flash all at once.

The pattern of emanation actually does resemble a lightning flash as it crisscrosses the sephiroth.

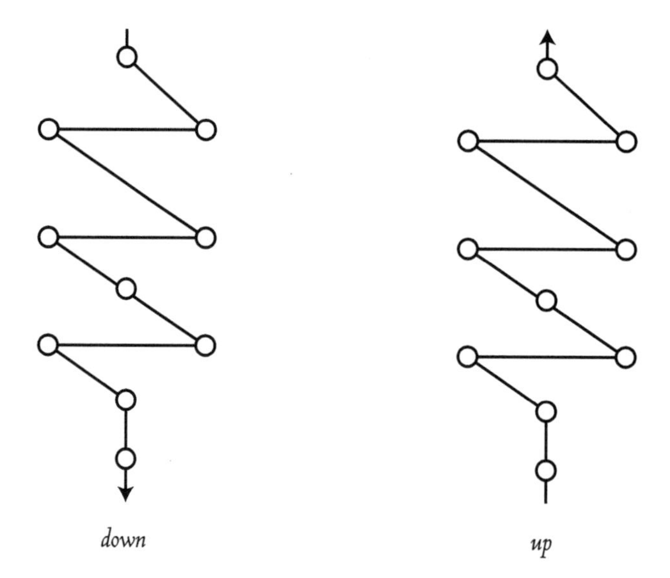

When we ponder how the world came into being, we picture the "lightning" of energy traveling down the tree. But if we wish to send our own consciousness toward a more direct encounter with that energy, then we visualize ourselves traveling up the tree.

The relationship of the sephiroth to each other suggests a sexual metaphor. In intercourse, the man gives his sperm into the woman. For life to begin, the sperm must meet with the egg that waits inside her. Eight of the sephiroth, Hokhmah to Yesod, express both male and female qualities. Thus they receive the energy from the sephirah above them, then give it in return to the sephirah below. In other words, even though

Hokhmah stands on the masculine pillar, and we call it the supernal father, it still takes on a female character when it receives the emanations from Kether. And even though we find Binah at the top of the female pillar, and we call her the supernal mother, she acts as a male when she gives the energy to Chesed.

Some will find this sexist, for it may seem to treat the female as a kind of empty vessel. And indeed, at the time these ideas originated, many people did believe that the sperm contained the entire human in miniature, the way a seed contains the entire plant. And just as the earth provides nourishment for the seed to grow into a plant, so people believed that the mother served only as the place for the fetus to grow until it was strong enough to leave the womb. (This idea probably originated in ancient Greece.) But just as we now know that no human fertilization can happen without the egg, so the sephiroth could not come into being and pass on the emanations without their own truth.

Two sephiroth do not act in this hermaphroditic way. Because Kether begins the tree, with no sephiroth above it, the Kabbalists consider it entirely male. And because no sephiroth come below Malkuth, it takes on an entirely female character. The Shekhinah, remember, dwells in Malkuth.

At this point, we might take a moment to look at an alternative view of the sexual imagery of the sephiroth. The traditional view is based on the masculine and feminine pillars, and their opposing qualities. But these qualities come from a patriarchal culture with a mistrust, even fear, of women. Many modern people question a system that considers maleness light, positive, active, loving, and merciful, and femaleness dark, negative, passive, harsh, and judgmental. It is not that anyone believes we should live in a world without harshness or severity. We know we need the dark along with the light. But we wonder why all the severe qualities go to women, especially when many people find their mothers more loving and expansive, and their fathers more restrictive and in charge of the rules.

Hermann Haindl's painting of the tree follows the traditional ideas but also goes beyond them. For most of the sephiroth, instead of specifically human qualities, we find animals, primarily snakes and birds, with largely ambiguous sexuality. By focusing on animals, Haindl returns the tree to a more primal state so that we may remember our own origins in nature. Where he does show human or humanlike figures, he often balances the sexual imagery. So in Binah, the sephirah of the supernal mother, we see a goddess-like figure rising out of the circle and looking to the light beyond Kether. But we also see that bearded flying rabbi reaching toward Hokhmah. And in Hokhmah, the supernal father, we see mostly owls, symbols of the sephirah's quality of wisdom but also feminine figures moving toward Binah. The owl itself traditionally belongs to female goddesses of wisdom.

We can call such images "cross-polarity," the mixing of male and female. And, in fact, we find a great deal of cross-polarity in Kabbalah, especially in the Western tradition. The Golden Dawn saw Netzach, on the male side of the tree, as the sephirah of the planet Venus, named for the goddess of love. Across from it, in the female sephirah of Hod, we find the planet Mercury, named for the god of intellect. Such a mixture of attributes may seem confusing at first, but it helps bring the tree to life. In nature and in ourselves the masculine and feminine "poles" never exist in isolation from each other.

Writer Judith Laura has suggested a fascinating way to recast the sexual imagery of the tree. She points out, first of all, that in ancient Israel tree worship belonged to a goddess, Asherah. Indeed, the Bible forbids planting groves of trees in holy places just because it will excite the followers of Asherah. Is it possible, Laura asks, that the Tree of Life symbolism originated in the ancient goddesses of nature? In Hebrew the word for "tree," *aytz*, is grammatically feminine.

This brings us to Laura's second point. In Hebrew, nouns are masculine or feminine, depending on their endings. Most of the sacred terms, including Kabbalah, Torah, and sephirah, are grammatically female. The names of the sephiroth consist of masculine and feminine words. Laura suggests that we not ignore these grammatical endings but instead see how the two principles take shape on the tree. When we do, we discover a fascinating balance. Kether is male, Hokhmah and Binah are both female (we will see in a moment that Hokhmah, wisdom, began as a female figure in both the Hebrew and Greek traditions). Chesed is male and Gevurah female, the same as in traditional Kabbalah symbolism.

Tiferet, however, is grammatically female, and so instead of a male "small face" looking up at a male "great face," we get a male/female balance between Kether and Tiferet. Netzach and Hod are both male, a balance to Hokhmah and Binah. Yesod, like Kether, is male, and Malkuth, like Tiferet, is female.

We thus end up with a tree that alternates, especially down the middle column, between male and female terms. The one place where we see the traditional right-left polarity is in Chesed and Gevurah. But these two sephiroth carry a special quality, for each one bears an alternative name. Chesed, mercy, also gets called Gedullah, or greatness, while for Gevurah, power, we also find Din, judgment. Chesed is masculine, but Gedullah is feminine. Gevurah is feminine but Din is masculine. This makes Chesed and Gevurah not just male and female, but rather male/female and female/male.

We might think of the gender-changing shamans in many cultures. In fact, Deuteronomy (chapter 22) specifically forbids men and women to wear the clothes, or carry objects, specific to the other gender. The priestly writers did not just want to reinforce sex roles. They opposed such play with gender specifically because people often switched roles in the worship of Asherah.

Here is how the tree looks with Judith Laura's grammatical "restoration."

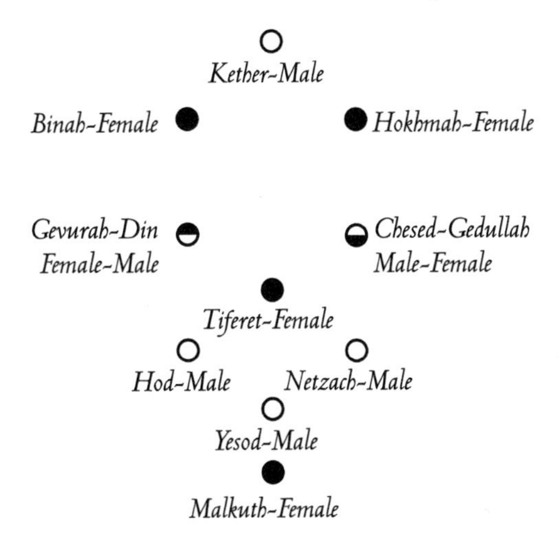

I do not mean to suggest here that we replace the Kabbalistic tradition, with its right and left pillars, with Judith Laura's more vertical sense of balance. We do not want to get rid of such a powerful set of ideas, with all the subtleties of meaning built up over millennia. Instead, as we consider the traditional masculine and feminine imagery, we simply might keep in mind alternative possibilities. As a way for humans to envision the divine, the Tree of Life rises out of very old roots, and there are many branches.

SIX

Ten Sephiroth, *Part I*

We have explored—paradoxically—the unknowability of the En Sof. We will now move into the tree itself, with Kether.

Kether

Kether represents undifferentiated energy. This means simply that it contains everything. Just as the En Sof contained all future reality (indeed all time as well as all space), so Kether contains the entire pattern of the tree, all the sephiroth with all their qualities. We might think of Kether as the monotheist idea of one god. In the modern view of this idea, we do not condemn or dismiss the various gods and mythologies of humankind. Indeed, the Golden Dawn and others have assigned any number of Pagan (as well as Christian) deities to the various sephiroth. Doing this, however, does not deny the oneness of God. Instead, it sees all these figures as expressions of that oneness, in the way the various sephiroth, with their many attributes, emanate from the wholeness and perfection of Kether.

In the last chapter, we looked at the traditional view of the sexual movement of the energy. Eight of the sephiroth seem to switch between maleness (giving energy to the sephirah below), and femaleness (receiving from above). Kether, we said, is entirely male, and Malkuth entirely female. This might seem to make these two sephiroth partial, or less developed, in the way a man who claims to possess no feminine qualities, or a woman who admits to no masculine, seems incomplete. Paradoxically, however, Kether and Malkuth are the most complete.

The eight sephiroth in the middle stand primarily in relation to the others. In a sense, they exist to give and to receive, to move the energy onward. But Kether contains everything within it, without any separation or distinction. Malkuth is the opposite, the place where everything goes. Malkuth, too, contains everything, and all of it in distinct reality.

Consider the names of the sephiroth. The eight internal sephiroth all bear titles of abstract qualities, such as wisdom, or beauty, or glory. Malkuth, however, means kingdom, a word that suggests the physical world. And Kether, the name for the most perfect sephirah, actually means crown, a completely real object (that goes with a kingdom). Kether is thus the most real, and realized, of all the sephiroth. We can imagine the crown of a king (the Kabbalists loved to envision God as a king on a throne), or even the crown of the human head.

The Haindl painting reminds us that until we can visualize all of the tree in such concrete terms we cannot entirely grasp its meanings. And it reminds us as well that the physical realities of nature constantly lead us to spiritual awareness. Kundalini yoga teaches us that when the life energy based in the spine moves up the chakras to the crown chakra—Kether—the head seems literally to open up, like a lotus flower. This is not a metaphor or concept but a physical sensation, for we lose our sense of isolation from the vast cosmos.

In Hermann Haindl's painting the bull's head fills most of the circle of Kether. The head is actually a skull. This does not suggest death, but only emphasizes the very ancient energy, like something we might find if we dig very deeply in a place undisturbed for millennia. Among the most archaic peoples, bulls and cows represented the physical embodiment of divine energy. Many mythologies describe a cow or buffalo or other female bovine as the first being, the creator. The Milky Way comes from her udders, and all the creatures from her body. The very solidness of cows and the great stream of their milk suggest the mother goddess.

Bulls embody the raw force of masculine energy. The image of bulls and their power goes back to the very beginnings of recorded civilization, and even prehistory. Bulls dominate many of the cave paintings in the European caves. In Lascaux, the most famous of the caves, with seventeen-thousand-year-old paintings, one picture of a running bull measures six meters. Bulls cover the ceiling of the central Altamira cave in Spain, so that the little girl who first discovered them, while exploring the cave with her father, was said to cry out, "Papa! The bulls! The bulls!"

The religious significance of bulls and cows may have developed partly from the shape of the horns. Curved into crescents, they evoke the waxing and waning phases of the moon, so that the sky, and the moon's cycles of birth, death, and rebirth, seem to have taken on life as powerful animals. In a similar way, the diagram and images of the tree give physical form to spiritual mysteries.

At the same time, the opposing crescents suggest polarity. We may think of male and female, positive and negative, over and under, good and evil. The tree contains such opposites in the right and left pillars. In Kether, however, these pillars have not yet emerged, and so we see both sides in the bull's horns. Energy passes between them, reminding us that duality is ultimately an illusion. Because of Kether's power, this energy generates great power, like an electrical storm.

Traditionally the left represents the female, the right the male. The painting, however, goes beyond such strict separation. Thus, on the upper left, we see that Einstein-like figure, and to the right of the bull's horns we can make out suggestions of a woman's face and long hair.

The bull and the horns form a diagonal upward to the left. In Hermann Haindl's iconography this angle moves us toward the sacred, for the left is the side of instinct and the unconscious. By comparison, a diagonal upward toward the right would move to the human, for the right is the side of rationality and consciousness.

Hokhmah

Kether begins the tree, so that all the distinct characteristics emanate from the crown. First of these is Hokhmah, the sephirah of wisdom. Hokhmah forms the top of the male pillar, with its qualities of expansion, compassion, and action. We see all these things suggested in the image of Christ on the cross. We do not actually see his face, but rather the crown of thorns. We also do not see the cross itself, but rather ropes seem to hold up his arms, as if to suggest the invisible divine energy that sustained Christ through his suffering.

Though the image of the Christian Son rises here behind Hokhmah, Kabbalist tradition refers to this sephirah as the "supernal father," the very principle of masculine creativity. If we remember the sexual metaphors prevalent in Kabbalah, we can describe Hokhmah as a kind of phallic outpouring that never empties itself, for its energy originates in the inexhaustible oneness of Kether.

Despite its primal maleness in Kabbalah, Hokhmah actually originated as a female mythological figure. The word appears in the Bible as a personified speaker, that is, a quality that speaks to the reader as a person. She comes to us most in the book of Proverbs. In chapter three, we read, "Happy he who has found wisdom, and the man who has acquired understanding . . . She is more precious than red coral, and all your jewels are no match for her" (this and the following quotations are from the New English Bible). In chapter eight, we read, "Hear how Wisdom lifts her voice, and Understanding cries out. She stands at the cross-roads, by the wayside, at the top of the hill."

Notice that Wisdom and Understanding—Hokhmah and Binah—seem to be one figure, a kind of divine female. In many ancient cultures, including Israel, goddesses were worshipped at both crossroads and hilltops. Still in chapter eight, Wisdom tells us, "The Lord created me the beginning of his works, before all else that he made, long ago. Alone, I was fashioned in times long past, at the beginning, long before earth itself." And, "When he set the heavens in their place I was there, when he girdled the ocean with the horizon . . . when he prescribed limits for the sea and knit together earth's foundations. Then I was at his side each day, his darling and delight . . . while my delight was in mankind." Here, Hokhmah existed before Creation, as God's consort. Wisdom has become a kind of cosmic figure.

And still more in chapter eight: "Wisdom has built her house, she has hewn her seven pillars; she has killed her beast and spiced her wine, and she has spread her table." Notice here the seven pillars, for the seven planets, the seven days of Creation, the seven lower sephiroth, and the seven double letters described in the Sefer Yetsirah.

The Greek philosophers also personified wisdom as a kind of goddess, called Sophia (an ordinary woman's name, of course, still in use today). The Christians made this figure a saint, Hagia Sophia. Caitlin Matthews, author of *Sophia, Goddess of Wisdom*, tells us that the philosophers took the images and qualities of ancient goddesses and abstracted them. Sophia was said to kindle the "inner fire within the soul" (Matthews). The study of wisdom—the word *philosophy*, or *philo-Sophia*, means "the love of wisdom"—was not simply an intellectual activity, the way we often think of it today. To truly become a lover of Sophia brings immortality, for we recognize the divine nature of ourselves and all creation. Matthews writes that some of the imagery associated with Sophia later went into the church's depiction of the Virgin Mary.

What should we make of the Kabbalist transformation of Hokhmah, what Judith Laura calls a "sex change"? Partly it reflects the tendency of patriarchal spiritual teachers to take over goddess qualities and designate them male. However, it also reflects the idea of Kether as beyond male and female. In the Bible, Wisdom and Understanding are one figure, a female lover of a male god. Kether establishes the first principle as before polarities. Hokhmah and Binah then emerge from Kether to create male and female.

Hermann Haindl's painting balances the polarity through a deliberate mixture of images. Three goddess-like figures stream out from Hokhmah toward Binah. They smile, as with the secrets and delights of that ancient figure of wisdom.

Within and above the circle we see three owls, the largest being within the sephirah itself. That large owl looks out at us with human eyes. Owls have represented wisdom in many cultures. The Algonkin Indians have called the owl the perfect "soul-bird." In Greece and Rome, before the age of the philosphers, the owl was the companion of the goddess most associated with wisdom, Athena-Minerva.

Owls symbolize wisdom because of their special qualities. They can turn their heads completely and look behind them, so that they seem to peer into the past and the future. They move silently, for a coating on their wings allows them to fly without any sound. The truest wisdom often seems to come to us without fanfare or announcement. In the famous saying of the Chinese sage Lao Tzu, "Those who know do not speak. Those who speak do not know." And owls fly at night, in darkness, so that they seem to embody mystery.

Esoteric wisdom often seems distant, or difficult, or even hard to believe. In fact, spiritual truth exists all around and inside us. Hermann Haindl's friend Gunther Cherubini tells a parable about this. Two fish meet and one asks the other if he knows anything about a substance called water. The other replies that he has heard of water, but doesn't believe it. It's just some occult fantasy.

Binah

From Hokhmah, the "lightning flash" of emanations moves across the tree to Binah. Charles Poncé describes the first three sephiroth as the development of true knowledge. Kether is knowledge itself, all that can be known. Hokhmah is the knower, the ability to look back at Kether and discover the truth. Hokhmah then looks forward to Binah, where the knowledge becomes realized and understood. Binah is that which is known.

Theoretically, we could go into deep meditation, race past all the lower sephiroth, contemplate Binah and Hokhmah, the mother and father, and by bringing them together experience Kether. However, Moses Cordovero and other Kabbalists warn against such radical action, for the power of Kether is too immense for us to come to it without careful preparation. Similarly, yoga teachers warn against exercises that will quickly raise the kundalini to the crown chakra for instant enlightenment.

Cordovero cited a famous passage from Deuteronomy to illustrate this. Chapter twenty-two (the same chapter that forbids cross-dressing), verses six and seven, tells us that if we find a nest with a mother bird sitting on her eggs, and we are hungry, we may take the eggs but leave the mother unharmed. The Torah then adds that if we do this, "You will have it good, and you will live long" (trans. Aryeh Kaplan).

This last statement suggests a magical quality, for why should treating a bird with mercy guarantee our own long life? Our understanding moves in a more mystical direction when we learn that the phrase "You will have it good, and you will live long" appears only one other place in the Torah, after the commandment to "Honor your father and your mother."

We can understand the "father and mother" as Hokhmah and Binah, the divine father and mother of existence. Honor these principles and we will live long and well. By the same kind of mystical interpretation, Moses Cordovero understood the mother bird we must not touch as Binah, and the eggs we may take as the seven lower sephiroth. He also wrote of the seven as "shields" against the overwhelming light of the upper triangle of Kether-Hokhmah-Binah.

Before Cordovero, the Zohar, in its wonderful allegorical way, declared that the messiah would come out of a "bird's nest" in Eden. Kabbalists have understood Eden here to mean Hokhmah, and the bird's nest, once again, to mean Binah. With Hermann Haindl's subtle crossing of images we find birds—the three owls—in Hokhmah. They do not move, however, but only perch in their perfect nest of wisdom. Later in the tree we find birds that move, especially the bird that literally flies toward us out of Tiferet.

The biblical passage about the bird's nest figures in another aspect of mystical history. A famous story tells of four rabbis who entered Paradise. Three of the rabbis could not assimilate the awesome experience and came to a bad end, while only Rabbi Akiva (whose name we've encountered before) entered and departed in peace. We can think of the rabbis in terms of the elements. Akiva, as earth, contains all the others and so can encounter the divine power of Paradise and then return to the ordinary world. The others represented the extreme of one element and so, unbalanced, could not integrate what they learned. The first rabbi looked at the divine radiance and died. We can call this an excess of fire. The second went mad from the experience. He represents water.

The third rabbi, named Elisha ben Abuyyah, was said to have seen two heavenly thrones rather than one and so lost his faith in Israel's one god. If we can think of him as the element of air, which represents the quality of intellect, then we might say he took what he saw too literally, and indeed had believed too literally in the doctrine of monotheism. He could not adjust to the subtleties of mystical revelation.

These were all historical figures, not just characters in a story, and in fact Elisha ben Abuyyah, a great scholar of his time, did lose his faith and become an enemy of his people. The more mundane version of how this happened is in some ways more mysterious than the Paradise story, for it involves both the commandment to honor our parents and that passage telling us we may take the eggs but must not harm the mother. Ben Abuyyah was walking with friends when he saw a father tell his son to climb a tree and bring back eggs from a nesting bird. The son did not want to do this but he obeyed his father. He reached the branch with the bird, and just as the Torah says, he took the eggs but left the bird. On the way down, he fell to his death.

Ben Abuyyah was stunned. The boy had followed the exact two rules that promised he would "have it good, and live long" and yet, as if in direct mockery of the Torah, he died. The rabbi's friends tried to tell him to look at the biblical passages in other ways; "have it good, and live long" could refer to life after death in the heavenly realm. But ben Abuyyah would have none of it. The fact is, he already had been questioning his faith due to a long study of Greek philosophy. If real life could prove the Torah blatantly false, then all of Judaism was a fake.

Once again, the problem was literalism. He could accept the complexities and depths of Greek thought, but needed his religion to remain literally true. This sad story illustrates the dangers of simplistic approaches to Kabbalah. Just as Moses Cordovero warns we must not try to "take the mother"—penetrate the mysteries of Binah—without great preparation, so we cannot truly enter the wonders of the Tree of Life if we expect to find all the meanings and correspondences and diagrams literally true. We need to think like the Zohar, in symbols and allegories and "mysteries of mysteries."

As the Great Mother, Binah gives birth to all that comes after, the seven lower sephiroth with all their qualities. But as any human mother will know, birth is not an easy experience. One reason Binah begins the pillar of contraction is because of the narrowness of the birth canal, the sense that we must pass through constrictions in order to be born, spiritually as well as physically. Once again, we might think of Max Siblo-Landsman's story of Moses's parting of the sea in Egypt, that the hand of

God reached down to part the thighs of a pregnant woman for the Hebrew people to be born into freedom. The waters are the birth water that must break for any baby, and Egypt—the Hebrew word for Egypt, *mitzrayim*, literally means "the narrow place"—becomes the birth canal of Binah.

The astrological tradition links Saturn to Binah. As the outermost planet, Saturn limits us so that we must learn to work within our limitations, to discipline ourselves. Doing so, we ultimately can transcend our limitations, for Binah is not the final point on the tree. Hokhmah and Kether lie beyond it. Isabel Radow Kliegman, in her book *Tarot and the Tree of Life*, gives a slightly different version of astrological links. She agrees with Binah as Saturn. But she describes Kether as the cosmos, and Hokhmah as the "infinite expression" of the zodiac. Saturn as Binah becomes the first place where a specific planet, or planetary sphere, takes shape. (Medieval cosmology taught that the soul travels through successive planetary spheres, Saturn to Jupiter and so on, until it reaches Earth and the fetus it will animate. The configuration of each planet against the zodiac as the soul passes through that sphere gives the astrological chart its special character.)

This, too, is a limitation, for it takes that infinite expression and narrows it to one planet. And yet without those specific planetary influences astrology would be meaningless. We could not have individual charts if everyone simply experienced the same totality. Thus, the expansion of Hokhmah must give way to the contraction of Binah. When we are born, our souls come from beyond into a body. We, too, pass from infinite possibility to a narrow reality. But this enables us to exist as individual people.

Binah completes the top triangle of the tree, the triangle beyond the abyss. We can think of Binah as the first place the energy from the En Sof rests before it travels on. Thus it represents an end as well as a beginning. We can think of this idea in less abstract terms if we realize that Binah brings death as well as birth. Death is inevitable in life, so we might say that when our mothers give us birth they give us our death at the same time.

In the 1980s, when the revival of goddess worship became a popular religion, people often criticized goddess worshippers for ignoring the harshness of the world. Followers of the goddess supposedly saw all reality through the soft lens of a loving Great Mother. But the opposite was true, for the goddess movement always pointed to the dark face of the death goddess as the other side of the mother. Binah, too, expresses both sides, not as opposites but as one energy.

With birth comes responsibility and karma, for we cannot escape the constant need to act and make choices. Thus, Binah begins the column of justice. The seeming separation of the two pillars sometimes makes us think that love and justice oppose each other. But remember, there is one tree, one energy that emerges in different ways, separates but always comes back together. Deeply ingrained in us we find a love of justice. As much as compassion, and mercy, come naturally to us, we also cannot bear to see injustice triumph, even if it occurs somewhere on the other side of the world.

Hokhmah and Binah both come from Kether, while Chesed and Gevurah, the lower aspects of the supernal father and mother, will return together, and intertwine, in Tiferet. The tree shows us divine qualities that at first glance seem far removed from our own lives. But as we look closer we discover that the tree also reveals our own nature. We see ourselves mirrored in the tree, for the Creator made us in the divine image.

One of the hidden truths of Binah as mother of life and death is the way our own lives transform into symbols and meaning. Essayist Callan Williams puts it this way: "The moment we're born, our bodies start to decay, and our stories start to grow." She goes on to say that to live a successful life means to leave behind a meaningful story by the time that we die. We might say that we enter into physical bodies just so we can understand that transformation of our lives into stories. This is one of the secrets of Kabbalah and all symbolic traditions.

Someone else who understands this truth is comic book writer Alan Moore, whose series *Promethea* forms one of the more elegant explications of Kabbalah in modern times. Promethea is a living story, originally a little girl whose father (a magician in ancient Alexandria, home of Hermes Trismegistus and the Emerald Tablet) sent her into the "Immateria," the world of myth. In later centuries humans who imagine her very intensely actually become different versions of her. Promethea tells one of her adversaries, "I am the holy splendor of the imagination. I cannot be destroyed."

In Moore's story, Promethea travels up the Tree of Life, from Malkuth to Kether, giving Moore a chance to vividly dramatize the sephiroth so often described only as intellectual concepts. Moore's own inspiration comes primarily from the work of Kabbalist and magician Aleister Crowley. Thus, some of the points attributed here to Alan Moore derive from Crowley and other, older sources. But Moore gives them a contemporary, immediate quality, using the visual medium of comics to bring the tree to life—a little like Hermann Haindl. Following Crowley, Moore emphasizes the sexuality of Binah. She appears as the divine mother—epitomized in Mary, the mother of Christ—but also as the whore of Babylon.

She calls herself "whore" because humans, especially men in a patriarchal culture, see the sexuality of women as fearful and dangerous. Unlike male sexuality, which rises and falls, the desire of women, once aroused, can seem unstoppable. This is partly why so many patriarchal cultures do everything possible to control women. We have all heard of the harsh restrictions of the Taliban in Afghanistan. But how many people know that in ancient Athens, the supposed birthplace of democracy, women literally could not leave the house without their husband's permission? These are just some of the ways men try to control Binah. In reality she cannot be controlled, for the female principle is eternal, "God's third head," as Alan Moore calls her.

Hermann Haindl pays tribute to the goddess in Binah with the image of a graceful woman rising up from the sephirah. She looks upward, serenely, as if she can see past Kether into the En Sof. Her belly swells, as if pregnant, but instead of a baby we see that rabbinical figure, its arms out as it reaches toward the female faces streaming from Hokhmah. Left is the side of instinct and the unconscious, right the side of reason and consciousness.

These may seem completely opposite, as polarized as male and female. The painting, however, suggests something more complex. Reason has its roots in the unconscious, while instinct emerges from consciousness. Without the depth of the unconscious, reason becomes nothing more than logic games without connection to the world. And the more conscious we become, the more we can recognize our instincts. In the spiritual world the male comes out of the female, the female out of the male. This world does not just exist somewhere far away, in "heaven," but in each one of us, for we are all the divine hermaphrodite. We simply choose not to recognize it.

Look to the left of the sephirah. A shadowy male face glances sideways. Could this represent all those Kabbalist masters who sought to comprehend the higher sephiroth through the "sideways" explorations of myth and meditation?

Despite all the movement and energy around her, the woman who rises from Binah stands serenely. An aura rises from her head. In Christian Kabbalah she is Mary, the queen of heaven. This divine Mary takes on the sorrow of the world, and her son's sacrifice (on the other side of the tree), for her Hebrew name is Miriam, whose name means the bitter saltwater of tears and the sea.

Miriam is also the name of the sister of Moses. Called a prophetess in the Bible, Miriam led the Israelites in celebration after the waters parted and they crossed the Sea of Reeds to freedom. Thus, she is both the mother who gives birth to the people (in Max Siblo-Landsman's story) and the consciousness that celebrates that birth. And she also takes on the sorrow of her children. These are the qualities of Binah.

Da'ath

Binah completes the upper triangle of supernal sephiroth. From Binah the energy moves across the abyss, the place of Da'ath, to the lower seven, beginning with Chesed. Hermann Haindl's painting does not show a specific circle for Da'ath. We do see a green lizard, or perhaps a salamander, climbing up the tree where Da'ath would be. It moves from the snakes of Chesed and Gevurah to the human images of Hokhmah and Binah. In evolutionary terms, lizards symbolize the oldest, most instinctive parts of our brains (see chapter eight, path 29). And yet its instinct moves it upwards, toward divine consciousness.

We have already discussed Da'ath in some detail and so we will not rest too long here. Alan Moore describes it as the place where God enters the physical world. This makes sense in mythic terms, for the three upper sephiroth represent the divine, while the lower seven symbolize the seven days of Creation. It also makes sense in esoteric psychology, for if the word "da'ath" means sexual knowledge, and if sex and spirit are the same energy in different forms, then Da'ath signifies the transformation of "higher" spirit energy into "lower" sexuality.

This knowledge is "forbidden," not to create an arbitrary rule (as the Bible story seems to suggest) but for our protection. It is one thing to speculate, and even ponder, about the place where pure divine energy enters into physical matter, but something else entirely to try to experience it. If we think of the movement upward on the tree, then Da'ath becomes the place where the physical literally disappears, like the giant stars that collapse into black holes. Da'ath is dangerous because once we enter it we cannot come out the way we were. We cannot return but must travel through it to emerge on the other side of the abyss.

Isabel Kliegman describes Da'ath as an "uncreated" sephirah, an idea that implies the tree is, in fact, unfinished. God, says Kliegman, expects us to complete this last place on the tree. We will do this when we learn to bridge the gap between the higher and lower triangles, between above and below, so that they do not just mirror each other ("As above, so below") but truly become one energy.

In Alan Moore's version of Da'ath everything gets turned inside out, including the strict separation of male and female that seems to rule the tree, with its right and left pillars. Male magicians become women as they pass through the mysteries of Da'ath.

If we think of the movement upwards on the tree (the direction of human attempts to comprehend the higher levels), then perhaps the male and female of Chesed and Gevurah get turned around in the "hidden" sephirah, only to emerge once more on their proper right and left pillars of Hokhmah and Binah. In the Haindl painting, however, we have seen how the male and female energies combine and blend into each other in the upper level. Symbolically, we might describe this as the effect of consciousness passing through Da'ath.

One more comment from Alan Moore before we leave the abyss once and for all. Moore considers what number we might assign to Da'ath. We can think of it as the eleventh sephirah, but eleven does not come between three and four. Instead, he says, we can call it pi, the Greek number considered magical since the time of Pythagoras.

Pi is actually a ratio between a circle's circumference and its diameter. Whatever the size of the circle this ratio always comes down to the fraction 22/7, twenty-two divided by seven. If you try to do the division you can never get a final answer. Instead, you get a decimel that goes on and on, forever, a fitting symbol of Da'ath's black hole of knowledge. The answer begins, however, as 3.14, so that pi becomes a mystical, unending number somewhere between three and four—between Binah and Chesed. Pi is a Greek letter, written like this: π. If we remove the curving "roof" of the letter, we get a close resemblance to the modern numeral 11.

Twenty-two divided by seven. Do those numbers sound familiar? Twenty-two is the number of pathways on the Tree of Life, one for each Hebrew letter (and Tarot trump card). Seven is the number of planetary spheres, as well as the seven lower sephiroth, and seven days of Creation, and the seven double letters in Hebrew. Does the Hebrew alphabet, and the Sefer Yetsirah, contain the secret of pi? If so, they do not reveal it directly. We might think of it as exactly the kind of hidden knowledge contained in the dark sephirah of Da'ath.

Chesed

Having passed through such mysteries, we come to Chesed, the sephirah of mercy. Chesed is the first day of Creation, when God separated the light from the darkness. We use the term "day" loosely here, for in the biblical account the sun and moon do not appear until the fourth day, Netzach. And of course, we know from modern science that the entire solar system did not come to life until very long after the Big Bang. Like so much else in Kabbalah, the seven "days" of Creation do not mean twenty-four-hour cycles, but stages—in other words, the sephiroth.

In Chesed the divine energy of pure being first enters into physical existence. Think of numbers and geometry. Number one, Kether, is a point. If you recall your geometry lessons, a point has no dimension. This is because Kether encompasses everything and so cannot be limited to any place. The number two connects one point with another, so that we discover the single dimension of direction, with a sense of purpose. Three gives us the possibility of three points and therefore different directions, but on a flat surface, a plane.

Only when we get to four do we find the possibility of height or depth as well as surface. With four, in other words, physical reality becomes possible. Think of pyramids. They appear triangular, but if you imagine holding one in your hand you will realize a pyramid consists of four sides, the bottom plus the three that rise upwards to the point. So four, Chesed, brings the possibility of reality. We will see in a moment that the harshness and strictness of Gevurah comes because it introduces the dimension of time, with all its possibilities of change and decay.

We have used the terms "supernal father and mother" for Hokhmah and Binah. The word "supernal" means grand principles, beyond our normal comprehension. Chesed and Gevurah also represent a divine father and mother, but in more immediate senses, with qualities we can more readily apply to our lives. Biblically, we can think of Hokhmah and Binah as Abraham and Sarah, while Chesed and Gevurah will refer to Isaac and Rebecca.

Kabbalists sometimes refer to the four letter name of God, Yod-Heh-Vav-Heh, as Father, Mother, Son, and Daughter. The Son and Daughter, however, act as more approachable parents to humans here below, as we struggle with existence. Some Native American tribes encompass this idea with the titles Grandfather, Grandmother, Father, and Mother. The first two represent the grand principles, the second two the gods and goddesses to whom we pray and give thanks.

The idea of generations of gods—or qualities—is certainly not unique to Native Americans, or Kabbalah. In many cultures we find the idea of a first generation who dwell beyond human comprehension, and a second generation who directly affect the world. In Egyptian mythology, Ra and Nut, the sun and the night sky, remain aloof and distant. Under their indifferent rule, humanity remains raw and barbaric. Nut's children, Isis and Osiris, bring civilization, including the invention of agriculture and cities.

Those who know the Haindl Tarot will remember Hermann Haindl's elegant way of expressing these ideas. His court cards all depict goddesses and gods from different cultures (India for Wands, Europe for Cups, Egypt for Swords, and Native America for Stones). At the same time, the cards bear the titles Mother, Father, Daughter, and Son (unlike the Kabbalah, Hermann gives primacy to the female).

The Mother signifies the oldest, most archaic expression of the divine, the source of life as understood in different cultures. The Father shows that primal force developed as a large religious idea. The Daughter and Son then involve themselves in humanity, and so they symbolize our own responsibility to live life in a meaningful way.

Chesed tops the pillar of mercy and expansion in the lower seven sephiroth. The Golden Dawn identified it with the planet Jupiter and the sky gods of various religions, such as Zeus, Jupiter, Indra, and Thor. To our limited senses the sky goes on forever, gentle, expansive, stretching into heaven itself. Of course, we can get hurricanes and lightning from the sky, but the overall effect is gentle and protective. From the sky we get the air that keeps us alive at every moment. Remember that so many words for *spirit* or *soul* literally mean "breath."

Gevurah will remind us of the harshness of life, but here in Chesed we revel in the sense that the cosmos loves us, and will protect us and help us as our souls journey through experience. When New Age people say "The universe will take care of you," or "Ask the universe for what you need," they are invoking Chesed. The astrological planet is Jupiter, large and expansive and, of course, the embodiment of the sky god.

Patriarchy identifies this protective, loving, expansive quality with fathers. Americans may recall a popular television show called "Father Knows Best," in which the wise and gentle father guided his children (and often his wife). Today, many people will find this description of fathers as the representations of love and mercy difficult to accept, not because they distrust fathers but because they wish to recognize mothers. If readers like, they can see Chesed and Gevurah more as principles and less as fathers and mothers.

In the Haindl painting the world of Beriah, Creation (Chesed, Gevurah, and Tiferet) is a world of what mythologist Joseph Campbell called the Animal Powers. The snakes and birds do not really represent the ordinary animals of nature. Instead, they signify divine forces, kinds of energy symbolized by different kinds of beasts. Those who have studied shamanism will think of the animal "allies" the shaman finds on her or his journey. But the tradition is far from unknown in Europe. Especially among the Greeks, but even in Christian times, snakes and birds have held a special place as representations of divinity.

The power of snakes in world mythology is so widespread that it constitutes a psychological mystery all by itself. Snakes fascinate humans with a primal power. Partly they represent rebirth, for a snake grows by periodically shedding its old skin and emerging fresh and young-looking, as if rejuvenated.

A snake tempts Eve in the Garden of Eden. Later, however, Moses will turn his stick into a snake, and then God will tell him to create a "brazen serpent" to carry at the head of the Israelites as they travel through the desert. This serpent of God heals the sick. The Hebrew word for snake, *nachash*, has the same letters as the verb "to divine." The numerical value for nachas is the same as the letters in *moshiach*, "messiah."

If snakes are mysterious, birds are almost transparent in their meaning. Beautiful to look at, they sing varied and melodic "songs." Most important, they fly, so that we can imagine them traveling to the heavens and communicating with the gods.

A dove brings an olive leaf to Noah so that he may know the flood has receded and life can begin again. Later, a dove brings the seed of God to Mary so that she might become pregnant with the divine child, the Christ.

The snake around Chesed belongs to the Greek tradition of the ouroboros, the snake that bites its own tail as a symbol of eternity, without end or beginning. Or perhaps we should say that the end is in the beginning, the tail in the mouth. We die, but our death only leads to new life. This is the essence of the sephirah of mercy, the realization that life never ends.

A long gooseneck curls up along the side of Chesed, as if to shelter it. In his comments on his painting, Hermann pointed out that the goose was an animal sacred to the Mother Goddess in northern Europe. Once again, we find the subtle mixing of polarities, for of course the goose appears on the right-hand, masculine pillar. It even rises to the right, and looks to the right, as if to emphasize the presence of the female within the male. We find the same thing above, with the owls in Hokhmah, for the owl is almost always associated with goddesses.

Below and on the left side of Chesed a skull emerges, only to subtly shift into a living face. The eyes look up slightly, toward Gevurah. The tail of the lizard in the area of Da'ath curls against the face. It creates a kind of border between the face and the flashing wings of the white bird in Tiferet. Like the snake, the skull and face teach the unity of death and life.

A precious stone shines from the forehead, in the place of the third eye. Hermann considers the opening of this psychic chakra another form of "mercy," for it enables us to see beyond our limitations. The face appears on the line from Chesed to Tiferet, connected to the Tarot card of the Hermit. This card emphasizes psychic wisdom and spiritual light (in the Haindl Tarot, the Hermit looks up toward a bright light; in older decks the Hermit carries a lantern). The third eye reveals these qualities to us as personal experience rather than doctrine.

Gevurah

From Chesed the energy moves across the tree to Chesed's partner, Gevurah. Gevurah brings in the dimension of time, and therefore decay and loss, but also the possibility of growth. It may seem to us that objects, like a table or a book, just exist, and time somehow passes around them. However, Einstein demonstrated that we cannot describe space and time as two separate qualities, but must talk of space-time. Thus, Gevurah completes the emergence of the divine energy into what we might call a usable form.

In Gevurah the expansive energy of Chesed takes shape. If it simply poured forth it would overwhelm existence. So Gevurah heads the lower pillar of contraction. Torah teacher Avigayil Landsman describes it as a diamond cutter. Chesed may produce beautiful raw gems, but until Gevurah cuts and shapes it and brings out all the facets we cannot appreciate the perfection.

Alan Moore describes Gevurah as the place where energy becomes purged of any impurities or weaknesses. As Moore has one of his characters (a street-tough angel) say, "It ain't that the universe is cruel or unkind, it just can't afford to get sentimental." Compare this to the New Age statement "Just ask the universe, it will give you everything you need." Both statements are true. The second is Chesed, the first Gevurah.

Kabbalists often describe Gevurah as the most severe place on the tree, a testing point. If we think of ourselves as traveling upwards on the tree (in a sense, back to our origins), then Gevurah becomes the place where we must shed our own weaknesses before we can revel in the overwhelming love and mercy of Chesed. This holds especially for the weaknesses we do not acknowledge in ourselves, those we keep hidden or deny, those we project onto others. It may seem unfair that we must pass through the harsh light of Gevurah before we can go to Chesed. But how can we accept the mercy of divine grace until we accept who we truly are?

As well as Gevurah, power, and Din, judgment, this sephirah sometimes bears yet a third name, Pachad, translated by the old expression, "fear and trembling." For the ego this can become a hard place, the dark night of the soul. For the spirit, however—our true selves—it becomes a great blessing, as wonderful as Chesed. Gevurah gives us the chance to free ourselves. We learn who we really are, and we learn to let go of our defenses.

The term Din, or "judgment," for the sephirah does not mean primarily that God, or some outside power, judges us. Instead, it gives us the ability to understand ourselves, and to make choices. Remember that this is the second day of Creation, when God separated the "waters above" from the "waters below." We invoke the adage "As above, so below" to remind us that our small lives mirror the cosmos and divine truth. But if there was no separation then we could not exist as individual beings.

A poignant story from the legend of the four rabbis who entered Paradise illustrates this. The second of the rabbis, the one who went mad, was named ben Zoma. Shortly after the event, a friend of ben Zoma's, another rabbi, was walking with his students when he saw ben Zoma standing by the road, a strange look in his eyes. Gently, he called to him, "Ben Zoma?"

The rabbi turned to him and said, "Between the waters above and the waters below there are only three fingerbreadths."

The rabbi turned to his students and told them, with great sadness, "Ben Zoma is gone." Several days later, ben Zoma died. Without the power of Gevurah to separate the waters, we ourselves cannot live. The overwhelming flow of Chesed will wash us away.

The Golden Dawn system (followed here by Haindl) attributes the planet Mars to Gevurah. We see a hint of this connection in the color red that suffuses the sephirah. The god Mars is harsh and masculine, the warrior. This will strike many as counterintuitive (to use a modern expression), the assignation of the god of war to the female pillar. Some describe it as a mixture of polarities, that is, to give the most masculine energy to the female side. Hermann Haindl also mixes polarities, perhaps more subtly, with his placement of images (for example, the female gooseneck alongside Chesed).

It will also become clearer if we know that many mythologies speak of ferocious warrior goddesses. Often, these are the same as the goddess of love, for all bring up great passion in humans. The Greeks tended to separate such aspects, with Aphrodite as love and Athena as warrior. But other cultures have linked them, such as Inanna of Sumeria, who was almost insatiable in her appetite for both sex and battle. Or Kali of India. Raphael Patai, in his book *The Hebrew Goddess*, has pointed to this link of love and war in an ancient Hebrew goddess, Anath, but even more in the Shekhinah. The Zohar describes this female aspect of God as a great lover yet always a virgin, as motherly and nurturing yet a ferocious warrior. We also might think of a mother tiger defending her cubs.

Some describe Gevurah as the link to the world of husks, or shells (in Hebrew *klipphoth*). Remember that in Isaac Luria's myth of the shattered vessels the holy sparks of the broken sephiroth flew back upwards to Binah, while the shards fell down into the world of dense matter. Mythologically, these shells are the source of evil, and of hell.

Alan Moore, in *Promethea*, gives us a more psychological perspective on this idea. The husks, he says, are what remains when we have allowed the sacred energy to drain out from any idea or experience. Religion without inner truth becomes repression. A marriage without love becomes a prison. Any activity without meaning becomes a shell. And life without meaning—without story, as Callan Williams might say—becomes a hell.

Fitting the harshness of Gevurah, Hermann Haindl's picture of it is simpler than that of Chesed. We do not see mysterious faces, or shadowy birds, along the sides of the sephirah. Instead, we get the vivid image of a nest of snakes. Looking more intense and fearsome than the single snake of Chesed, they intertwine with each other. Two of them are green, but one is much lighter than the other so that they can symbolize the mix of polarities, light and dark. They either bite or kiss each other—a fitting ambiguity for a sephirah that evokes the power of both passion and war.

The third snake, white, watches quietly. White is the color of Kether, the color that contains all qualities, for white light combines all the colors of the spectrum. If we follow the white snake's body we will see that it disappears behind the central pillar of the tree. We also will notice that the back of the snake is actually black. Once again, we find the union of opposites. The hidden side of white is black. The hidden sight of light is darkness.

The white/black snake is a king cobra, long seen as holy in India. In ancient Egypt the cobra, called uraeus, symbolized the divine power of the pharaohs. Partly, it represented the king's rule over the life and death of his subjects. It also may have reflected a special quality of cobras. In India, people extract the venom, dry it, and use it as a drug to induce sacred visions. Thus, like some mushrooms and other plants, the cobra becomes a "royal road" to knowledge of the divine.

For many, snakes can represent fear and punishment, qualities we might think of as part of Gevurah. However, the cobra here does not strike but simply looks on, with what Hermann Haindl calls a "magical element." Magic comes to us even in the narrowest, most constricted moments.

SEVEN

Ten Sephiroth, *Part II*

Continuing our journey on the Tree of Life . . .

Tiferet

We leave Gevurah and travel to the tree's center, its heart, Tiferet, the place of beauty. Tiferet represents the chest, the home therefore of the breath, which is divine; as we have seen, the word for *soul* or *spirit* in many languages literally means "breath." In Tiferet the life energy of existence passes in and out. When we breathe we share ourselves with the world, and it is in Tiferet that we breathe. Human beings need all our organs to live and be heathy, but three organs are vital to life continuing at all. These are the brain, the heart, and the lungs. The brain resides in Kether, the center of the highest triad. The heart and lungs live in Tiferet, directly below Kether, the focal point of the middle triad.

Earlier we described Binah as heart energy, for Binah means understanding and we cannot truly understand something if we do not experience it in our hearts. We also said that the Binah heart comes to dwell in Tiferet. This touches on a basic quality of the central sephirah, that of a meeting place of the above—that is, divine energy of the spirit—and the below, the physical world. The heart is a physical organ, pumping blood through the body. But it also focuses our emotions. We speak of sadness as a broken heart, and anyone who has gone through a painful loss will know that it really does feel like the heart breaks in the chest. When we're happy we say that the heart is full, or even that it can burst with joy. And we use the heart itself (or a simplistic drawing of it) as an icon of love.

Like all the sephiroth on the middle pillar, Tiferet balances the right and left sides. But Tiferet also balances above and below, so that it acts as the pivotal point for all qualities. We can imagine the tree turning about, with Tiferet as the still center, around which everything moves. Tiferet comes halfway between the pure and "unmanifest" (non-physical) energy of Kether, and the "manifest," or physical reality, of Malkuth. Between Malkuth and Tiferet comes Yesod, the power of imagination to go beyond the physical and so rise up to Tiferet. Between Tiferet and Kether, invisible Da'ath allows consciousness to know the ascent to that great unseparated wholeness of Kether. Move in any direction from Tiferet—up, down, right, left—and you tip the balance one way or another. But dwell in Tiferet and you live in peace and harmony, and energy both dynamic and still. And this is beauty.

In Jewish Kabbalistic mythology Tiferet becomes the "short face," or "lesser countenance," that looks up at Kether, called the "long face," or "greater countenance." These titles correspond to the first and third letters of God's four letter name, Yod-Heh-Vav-Heh (in one of the fascinating cross-polarities of Kabbalah, the Vav—the short face—actually is written like an extended version of the Yod—the long face). In a mystical tale by the great Hasidic teacher Nachman of Bratslav, the two "faces" become the son of a conventional rabbi and a Hasidic master. The son dreams that he must go see the master, but his father won't allow it. For him, such Hasidic *rebbes* (gurus) are charlatans. After the son's death the rabbi learns that if his son—symbolic of humanity's yearning—had met the master—God's compassion—face-to-face, then the messiah would have come to end our long exile from the full consciousness of God.

Tiferet is the third day of Creation described (metaphorically) in the Bible. On the third day God separated the land from the waters. In other words, what we think of as reality first emerges from the surging energy of the principles expressed in the higher sephiroth.

According to Charles Poncé, Tiferet's perfect harmony makes it the Great Androgyne, with both male and female qualities. Though primarily male, Tiferet has female breasts, as if to nourish the world. We might remember here that one of the Bible's common names for God—*Shaddai*, usually translated as "Almighty"—comes from the Hebrew for "breasts."

With her characteristic directness, Isabel Kliegman describes Tiferet as the meeting place of "brilliant energies" from above and the "good rich nutrients" of the earth. We grow in the nutrients of our physical reality and life struggles. These will only drag us down if they do not join with spiritual meaning. Out of this meeting we get beauty. We know this is true from art, for the best poems, songs, and paintings all find spiritual transcendence in human suffering.

In Tiferet soul and body, self and ego, higher consciousness and personality all join together. Tiferet signifies God's moral power coming down from above to meet the human ideal of an ethical life. We must reach up from our humanity to encounter the divine. The rabbis considered Jacob the representation of the ethical ideal. Thus we get Hokhmah and Binah as Abraham and Sarah, Chesed and Gevurah as Isaac and Rebecca—the next generation—and Tiferet as their son, Jacob. From Jacob and his wives Leah and Rachel—the two aspects of the Shekhinah—come the twelve tribes, symbolic of all humanity.

In Genesis, when Jacob wrestles with God, he becomes *Isra-el*, a name that literally means "God-wrestler." His people bear his name, Israel, because they come from his "seed" and the womb of his love, Rachel (whose name means "mother sheep of God," and who may originally have been an all-nurturing sheep goddess). We, too, are created, transformed, when our humanity struggles with our inner divinity.

In the story, Jacob and the divine being wrestle all night, but neither side wins; Kabbalistically, they wrestle in Tiferet, the place of balance. The significance of the story lies in the idea of struggle, for our ordinary consciousness doesn't just melt into divine energy. We grow out of the battle between the two. Alan Moore comments that Tiferet contains great sorrow as well as joy, for without sorrow the tree would not be heaven, it would be Disneyland.

Remember that Kabbalists sometimes call the tree, especially the extended tree of the four worlds, Jacob's ladder. Remember, too, that in that extended tree, Tiferet contains the Malkuth of the world above it and the Kether of the world below it.

In modern Kabbalah, Tiferet astrologically represents the Sun, whose radiant energy gives us life. Just as the sun stands at the center of all the other planets (something not understood until the modern era), so Tiferet stands in the center of the other nine sephiroth. This leads the Western tradition to identify Tiferet with all the sun gods of the world's mythologies, such as the Egyptian Ra and the Greek Apollo, both gods of light and reason. The sun signifies reason, because in the light of day all things become clear and understood. Hermann Haindl used Ra for the Father of Swords in his Tarot deck.

According to Israel Regardie, Tiferet also embodies gods of beauty. This idea may strike some as odd, for in modern culture we have separated beauty from masculinity and, indeed, to modern eyes images of these gods often appear effeminate. Similarly, the idea of the goddess of love as a warrior—one of the ways the Zohar describes the Shekhinah—seems almost unnatural to us. We believe that men fight heroically and women either adorn themselves for the men or else nurture their babies. Older cultures have allowed more of a mixture of these basic human qualities. And if we look at animals we will see that the powerful males display great beauty, the females great ferocity. Tiferet balances all such dualities.

The gods of beauty include Krishna, from India, whom Haindl painted as the Son of Wands in his Tarot deck. Krishna represents art and music and sensuality, yet also war, a blend of Chesed and Gevurah found in Tiferet. Other gods of beauty include the Norse Balder, whom all nature adored and promised never to harm, except for the lowly mistletoe; Adonis, loved by the goddess of love herself, Venus, whom the Golden Dawn saw in Netzach, the sephirah after Tiferet; Attis, god of the transsexual worshippers of Cybele, the Great Mother; and Dionysos, the god of ecstasy, who invented wine.

Many of these gods fill the role of a son, or a younger generation, in their mythologies. The sun gods, on the other hand, usually represent the father principle (the pun of son and sun is a nice coincidence). Again we see the Tiferet mixture, with the solar father energy descending from above and the human son consciousness rising up from below. In Kether the divine light remains a principle, beyond nature. In Malkuth the physical dominates. They meet in Tiferet in the image of the sun, a physical object made of burning hydrogen and helium, and yet a symbol of life and truth.

The gods of beauty are often gods of sacrifice and rebirth, dismembered or mutilated, killed, and then reborn in their eternal perfection. They embody, not just symbolize, the cycles of nature. In spring the beautiful flowers grow out of the body of the dark earth, their mother, brought to life by the sun, their father. They grow strong, only to wither and die in autumn and winter, then return again, just as the sun itself grows weaker and stronger with the season. Once again, Tiferet and its gods of beauty unite the principle of death and rebirth with the reality of the plants and seasons.

For Christian and Western Kabbalists the epitome of all these beautiful son gods who die and return is Christ. To Christians, Christ is both god and fully human. Orthodox Christian Churches consider this union a wholly unique event, beyond the scope of ordinary people. In these traditions we can, and should, imitate Christ, for he represents the ideal human (the way Jewish Kabbalists look at Jacob), but they would find it blasphemous to suggest we might somehow become the same as Christ, both human and divine. But not all Christians agree with this. When esotericists speak of "Christ consciousness," they are saying that anyone can achieve at least moments of awakening the presence of God in their own being. One way to do this is through contemplation of the tree, and the discovery of ourselves in Tiferet.

Christ signifies the union of above and below in a person. In Christian belief the crucifixion brings together eternity and history for, again, they consider the crucifixion a unique event, the one-time self-sacrifice of God in order to redeem the sins of humanity through all time. Compare this to the Pagan version of the beautiful God who dies and returns every year as the cycles of nature, without reference to sin.

There is a way to redraw the connections of the sephiroth that will illustrate some of these ideas, including the way Tiferet embodies both the principles of above and the realities of below. Because Da'ath is invisible (or uncreated, as Isabel Kliegman would say), we can link the first six sephiroth, Kether through Tiferet, in a circle. At the same time, the bottom five, Tiferet through Malkuth, form a cross. The revised tree looks like this:

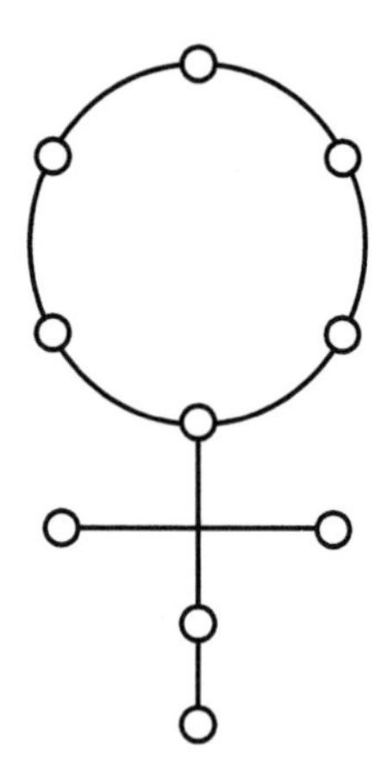

In symbolic tradition the circle represents the divine, perfect and without end, radiant. True circles exist in only three natural images: the sun, the full moon, and the pupil of the eye, the organ that beholds the heavenly bodies. The cross (or a square) signifies Earth, with its four directions. When people talk of "squaring the circle" as a very difficult task, they actually refer (whether they know it or not) to an ancient mathematical problem consisting of trying to create a square with the exact same area as a given circle. In fact, no one can do this, because unlike a square, with its straightforward measurements, the area of a circle contains the "irrational" number pi (you may remember, from geometry class, the formula πr^2 to determine the area of any circle, with r as the length of the radius). We can never calculate the inside of a circle as a concrete number because it always will include pi, that same "number" between three and four that Alan Moore suggested for Da'ath. (It is sad that our schools do not teach the esoteric side of geometry. More people might learn such subjects if they knew it all meant something.)

Thus the circle symbolizes heaven, and the square, or cross, Earth—two fundamentally different realms. Tiferet, however, exists in both. And if we place Christ on the cross, then we find his head in Tiferet, his arms on the line between Netzach and Hod, with the hands nailed to the sephiroth themselves, his genitals in Yesod, and his feet in Malkuth. The head is in heaven, the feet are in Earth.

The entire image forms the planetary sign for Venus, used in modern biology to symbolize the female. Here we see a truly elegant cross-polarity, and a reminder that trees were once worshipped as embodiments of goddesses.

It may seem that some of these symbolic systems do not precisely match each other. The tree contains the twenty-two letters/pathways, but also the circle and the square. Tiferet represents Jacob, and Christ, and sun gods, and gods of beauty. As Christ, Tiferet signifies his whole being, but also his head. The cross symbolizes the meeting of eternity and history, but also the material world, with its four directions.

We needn't worry about these seeming contradictions. The desire to match everything up in one neat system drastically limits our vision, for the true power of an image lies in its ability to symbolize many different things at once, each one true in itself. So, for example, we can see the sephiroth as one world, or all four. To learn to hold many meanings for the same image is the beginning of sacred consciousness. We also might call it an attribute of Tiferet.

Another double symbol—Tiferet represents the head of Christ, but also the heart of Adam Kadmon, the place where the divine understanding of Binah comes to rest in the body. In the human body the heart is the middle chakra, once again the border between above and below. The chakras below the heart embody (from the bottom up) survival, sexual drive, and "gut knowledge." Those above give us (from the top down) enlightenment, psychic awareness, and communication. We can see a clear difference here in the physical below, the mental and spiritual above. They meet in the heart, in Tiferet.

With so much complex symbolism for Tiferet, it is ironic, yet fitting, that Hermann Haindl should make this one of his simplest pictures (though not simplistic or naïve, qualities never found in Haindl's art). The bird flies directly toward us, as if to bring Tiferet off the painting and into our lives. Because the sephirah emphasizes so much the mid-point, with above and below and right and left at equal distances, it may seem static or even trapped, unable to shift in any direction. But staticness certainly is not the concept of Tiferet, in some ways the most alive of all the sephiroth. The bird suggests a third dimension—forward—so that the tree no longer appears flat or remote.

With its incredibly fast wings, and its needle-like beak, the bird resembles a hummingbird, an animal often considered sacred for its wondrous ability to hover in mid-air and then move at great speed, like a divine messenger. It is not actually any specific creature (like the swan, or the goose), but a spirit. Again we find that idea of the spiritual taking physical form in Tiferet. We might remember that in Christian tradition the Holy Spirit came to Mary in the form of a white dove.

For Hermann Haindl, a spirit-bird is not a one-time mythological creature. In the time they spent with Native Americans, Hermann and his wife Erica experienced the reality of such messengers, creatures that would physically appear in a ceremony or vision quest that people actually can touch. This is another way the painting brings the Tree of Life alive, by reminding us that "sacred" is not just a concept but a reality as present as an oak tree or a hummingbird.

The spirit-bird's wings are fine and delicate. Their great speed may remind us of what the spiritualists call higher vibrations, that is, realities beyond our normal senses. The eyes and the point of the beak shine black, as if to penetrate into deep mysteries.

Below Tiferet we see white birds, the swan coming out of Netzach, the wings above the mouth in Hod. Above Tiferet, and almost framing it, we find the snake tails that curve down from Chesed and Gevurah. On the left, the spirit wings actually touch the green snake tail. These snakes above and birds below form another example of Haindl's cross-polarities, for birds often signify heaven and snakes the underworld. In this painting, all the qualities move in and out of each other.

Though the light of Tiferet shines yellow, like the sun, shades and gradations move through the circle. We see darkness in the lower right, where the imagery of the tree will move on to the lower triad, beginning with Netzach. The inner surface of Tiferet actually appears like soft, ancient stone (a favorite motif in Haindl's art). Tiferet gains a more solid substance than any other sephirah in the painting, including Malkuth. The mixture of yellow light and rock makes Tiferet the philosopher's stone of the alchemists, that magical power that could transform lead into gold and bestow immortal life. How fitting for the center of the tree, where all the energy meets and comes to life.

Netzach

From the perfect balance of Tiferet the energy shifts in the direction of manifestation, what we call "the real world." Malkuth will embody physical matter itself, but before we get there we must pass through the lower triangle that points down to the physical. This triangle concerns the qualities of the ordinary world and human ways of expression. The top triangle gives us the great principles of Above—understanding, wisdom, and pure spirit. Now we come to the human qualities of Below—emotions, intellect, and imagination.

The Golden Dawn named Netzach "Eternity." Kabbalists also call it victory and endurance. If we think of ourselves as moving up the tree, we begin in the world of the conscious, Malkuth. We learn the lessons of our imagination in Yesod, analyze and study existence with our intellects in Hod, and then finally engage reality with our full emotions. Only this emotional openness will allow us to move on to Tiferet, the gateway to the higher realms. Despite the importance of intellect in discovering how the world works—without intellect we could never comprehend the complexities of the tree—intellect sets up a distance between ourselves and reality. This is why intellect comes in Hod, on the left-hand pillar of contraction. Our emotions connect us directly to existence. They open us up, without barriers. Therefore, we find these qualities on the right-hand pillar of expansion. Our emotions give us a glimpse of eternity.

Once again, we notice the cross-polarity, for in Western cultures we tend to think of intellect as male and emotion as female. In fact, in Western Kabbalah the planetary sphere for Netzach is Venus, the planet that belongs to the goddess of love. Diagonally up from Netzach (on the line through Tiferet) Gevurah contains the planetary realm of Mars, whose aggressiveness often seems the polar opposite of Venus. Yet Gevurah appears on the female side of the tree. We might think of this constant cross-polarity as the tree—the cosmos—fertilizing itself. We also might remember that just as we discovered the warrior goddesses of Gevurah, so we might recall gods of love in Netzach.

Netzach corresponds to the fourth day of Creation (remember, we are not suggesting that the universe actually came into being in six days). On day four God created the sun and moon, called the greater and lesser lights. These descriptions should make it clear that we are talking here of something besides the physical bodies in the sky. The greater light means Tiferet, whose solar consciousness allows us to look up toward Kether, at the same time that it shines down on the physical world. The lesser light is Yesod, whose lunar light opens the path of imagination and the unconscious. On the vertical middle column, Yesod comes between Tiferet and Malkuth. It reflects and filters the overwhelming light of the tree's center. Tiferet, Netzach, Hod, and Yesod form a diamond pattern on the tree.

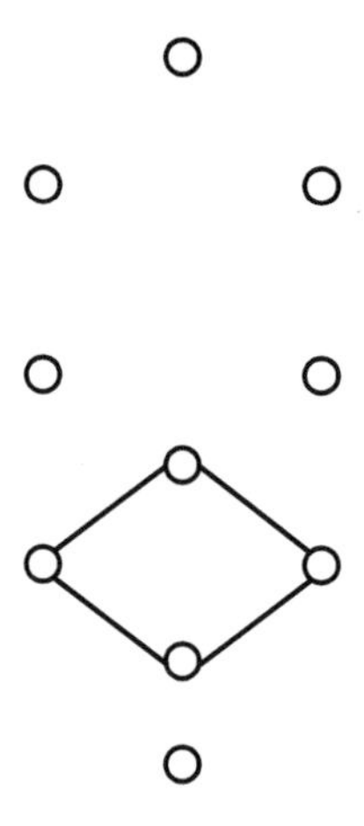

Remember, too, that the picture of the tree as a circle over a cross (♀) designates both women and the planet Venus (similarly, the planetary glyph for Mars, ♂, now represents men). We can say, then, that symbolically the sephirah of Netzach, the realm of love, contains the entire tree.

We spoke of human consciousness moving up the tree and going beyond intellectual concepts of Hod to the emotions of Netzach. But such movement is really backwards, since the energy actually travels "down" from Tiferet to Netzach and then to Hod. In fact, experience does match such movement, even if we believe that the opposite is happening. In other words, the emotions come first, even when we do not realize it.

We often seem to filter all our reactions to life through a set of preconceived ideas (a distortion of Hod). We meet people from some ethnic group and before we know anything about them we make assumptions of what to expect. This is an extreme example but we can think of many more. Even in romance, where emotions should rule, we make all sorts of intellectual judgments about a potential partner before we can really experience anything at all of the person.

But this is an illusion. Our emotions always come first, in any encounter with a person or life. The attempt to substitute prejudices or any pre-set ideas for direct emotional experience is simply an attempt to protect the ego from the raw, uncontrolled energy of emotion. And such "ideas" are not really intellectual at all, but a distortion, for genuine intellect—Hod—uses emotional experiences as data. It does not try to overrule them.

Netzach is the realm of water, just as Gevurah is fire. Where fire (on the left side of the tree) burns off impurities, seeking the essence, water flows over and through all of life. It engulfs and so embraces everything, without distinction. Water is love, for in fact love suffuses all emotion, even when we might characterize feelings as something else, such as anger, sadness, or hope. Love flows through everything.

The goddess Venus (Aphrodite in Greece) embodies our human understanding of love, especially sexual attraction. Some of the myths, such as Homer's descriptions of Aphrodite's dalliances, make love appear vain, or selfish, or silly. But these are just human projections of our own failings onto the divine images. Sexual energy is so fundamental to our existence we have trouble accepting its full power.

Alan Moore points out that attraction holds the universe together. Electricity works through the attraction of positive and negative poles, often compared to male and female energy. Two forces hold together the very atoms of existence, the strong force in the nucleus and the weak force that keeps electrons in "orbit." At the other end of the scale, gravity keeps the stars and planets in their pathways, a mutual relationship that acts across unimaginable distances. We are used to thinking of these forces or laws as cold and unemotional. But why should we assume that no trace of eros or passion runs through the world, when we know how strongly it runs through us? If "As above, so below," then why not see the cosmos as sexual? Let yourself think about this and see how it changes how you look at the world (not to mention your high school science class).

In the Haindl painting, a swan flies from Netzach toward the intellectual realm of Hod. Its long neck stretches out for its head and beak to cross the middle pillar, while its right wing reaches above into Chesed. For its beauty, and its ferociousness, the swan was sacred to the goddess of love. Swans drew Aphrodite's chariot through the sky. For Haindl, the swan represents the magic of nature, that such beautiful creatures exist in such a harsh world. Haindl paints the swan in a straight line, with its right wing up and its left wing across its body so that nothing of the bird points down. Its perfection has freed it from earth. It evokes the "eternity" that the sephirah embodies. Individual swans are born, grow, and die, but the loveliness of swans live forever. The green of the sephirah suggests this eternity within the cycles of nature.

Below the sephirah we see the bottom of the right-hand column of mercy. It appears as old stone, with various animal heads and eyes all merged together. In the dark area to the right of the pillar we see a shadowy face, with what seems to be a jewel in the place of the third eye. To the left of the bottom of the pillar, wedged between the pillar and the neck of the lamb in Malkuth, appears an ancient pitted rock that resembles the skull of some animal. All these creatures and rocks sliding into each other evoke one of Hermann Haindl's great themes, that over time everything in nature transforms and merges together. In the consciousness of eternity, God's statement to Adam, "You are dust, and to dust you shall return," becomes not a condemnation but a simple truth. We come out of nature, we return to it, and from our bodies something else will emerge.

Hod

Across the tree we find the bottom sephirah on the pillar of judgment, Hod. Hod, glory, is the sephirah of intellect, the faculty that indeed judges. Without Hod to restrain the Netzach quality of endless love we would find ourselves tossed wildly on the seas of emotion. Aphrodite's greatest acolyte, the poet Sappho, wrote of the goddess's passion, how it sweeps us away like a leaf in a storm. Yet Sappho herself used one of Hod's deepest attributes, language, to convey her experience of love. Without Hod's intellect Sappho could not have stepped back from her passion to compose poems of such intense emotion, and at the same time such elegance (part of Hod's contribution to art), that they have inspired readers for thousands of years.

Isabel Kliegman describes Hod as "the logical thinking mind" that balances the overflowing emotions out of Netzach. One reason we call this sephirah Glory is because the mind is humanity's glory, our great strength that enables us to survive and flourish in a world of dangers and hardships. If we go too far in this direction, if we let logic rule us entirely, we can change our lives to a waterless desert, without emotion. Once we do that, we can fall prey to illusion, such as a skepticism that denies life's wonders, or a pointless cleverness.

But Hod represents far more than logic. As the mind, it signifies invention, brilliance, the ability to make sense of all the complicated experiences that have come before it. Hod is the fifth day of Creation, when all the variety of creatures came into being. Only the intellect can comprehend and find order in the almost unimaginable proliferation of species that populate the world.

We find Hod on the left side because it receives the energy of Netzach. But Hod is not passive, any more than a woman is passive because she "receives" a man's sperm and grows a child inside her. Hod's glory is to shape and structure and find meaning in Netzach's flood of spiritual Eternity.

To Western Kabbalists, this is the realm of the planet—and the god—Mercury. The closest planet to the sun, Mercury has the shortest orbit, and moves the fastest. This gives it the quality of swiftness. Think of the image of the god Mercury, with his winged helmet. Mercury is a male deity, and we commonly think of mental activity as masculine. Once again, we get that crossing so common on the tree, for we find Aphrodite on the masculine pillar and Mercury on the feminine. The Greeks called the god of mind Hermes (the same name as Hermes Trismegistus, author of the Emerald Tablet). If we combine Hermes and Aphrodite—masculine and feminine powers, Netzach and Hod—we get the word hermaphrodite, a person with the reproductive power of both sexes (compare this to the description of Tiferet as "the Great Androgyne").

If mind represents the glory of humanity, then language becomes the true jewel in that crown. Language allows us to convey our thoughts person to person, but also generation to generation, through writing and oral traditions. Writing, too, is an attribute of Mercury. The Egyptian Hermes, called Thoth, was the inventor of writing. His standard image shows him with a sheet of papyrus, in the act of scribing. The Norse god Odin, called Wotan in Germany, brought the runes, the magic alphabet, to humanity. The name *Wotan* gives us the English name for the middle day of the week, Wednesday, dedicated to the planet Mercury.

The runes are not magic because of some special origin (though they do originate in the dark well at the base of Yggdrasil, the Norse Tree of Life). All alphabets are magic. The Sefer Yetsirah describes how God created the world with the power of letters. For Kabbalists, therefore, the Hebrew alphabet existed before the world. The letters formed the Torah, the blueprint of Creation, described by mystical Jews as "black fire on white fire."

The Hebrew letters form the pathways between the sephiroth, first delineated by Moses Cordovero. These pathways are the very rungs of Jacob's ladder. Because there are twenty-two of them we get multiple possibilities on the tree, instead of just one lightning flash to go from sephirah to sephirah. From Tiferet alone you can travel to every sephirah but Malkuth (Yesod comes between Tiferet and Malkuth). For Western Kabbalists (though not in the Jewish tradition) the Tarot cards have become a pictorial representation of the letters and their pathways. The twenty-two Tarot trumps, called the Major Arcana, allow us to follow the paths with the aid of visual symbols. Each Tarot card becomes like a bottomless well that we can look into our entire lives and still find new things.

Most primal of all is language itself. In the traditions of Israel, India, and Egypt, the original God, the eternal divine being, literally spoke the world into existence. In Genesis, the first act of Creation is the statement "Let there be light."

For humans as well, language is creative. Our words do not simply record observations or feelings. Language orders the chaos of existence. It lets us comprehend how things fit together, and then share that with others. And language evokes and stimulates. As anyone who reads poetry knows, language can induce different emotional states, surprise and excite us. Though the ultimate mystical experiences lie beyond words, language can help us grasp at least the sense of what happens when the journeyer goes beyond self to encounter the divine. Lao Tzu wrote, "Those who know do not speak. Those who speak do not know." And yet that statement is made out of words.

Some Kabbalists call Hod "splendor." Alan Moore writes, "Language gives a shape to the splendor of the intellect" (*Promethea*, issue 15). Because he is telling a story, a comic book in which his character Promethea journeys up the tree, Moore brings in Mercury himself to speak to us. At one point, Mercury turns and looks toward the reader, to tell us that sometimes the gods live inside the stories we tell about them. Gods—the god Mercury tells us—are abstract essences clothed in language, image, and story.

Like the element Mercury, our thoughts shift and flow and change shape constantly. Anyone who has tried to clear the mind in meditation will recognize just how slippery—and insistent—our thoughts are. We can build great wonders with our minds, yet our thoughts themselves are more unreal than the invisible air. Like the mind, the god Mercury rules over many activities—both prudence and cunning, science and invention, but also frauds and swindles. Mercury, like thought, can move between the worlds, from the upper realm of the gods to the daily life of humans to the dark underworld of death. Mercury is the messenger of the gods, a title we might consider for the mind. The mind composes thoughts and sends them "on high," as the Jewish Kabbalists say, and the mind receives "intimations of immortality" (a phrase from the English poet Wordsworth) that put us in touch with divine reality beyond our daily lives.

Israel Regardie writes of Hod as the "lower plane" of Hokhmah (notice that it shifts to the left side of the tree, the female side). Its color, orange, mixes the red of Gevurah with the yellow of Tiferet. In the Hermann Haindl portrayal of Hod we see a partially open mouth with a hint of a smile. It could be saying something, or perhaps has just said it. We can see the act of speech, but we cannot see the words. We can only imagine the message.

Above the mouth, as if to hide the face, we see white wings but not what bird belongs to them. In conversation about this sephirah, Hermann Haindl suggested they might belong to the great archaic Goddess, whose name is forgotten even as her birds remain. Tiferet, Netzach, and Hod form a triangle of white wings, a triangle that points upward toward the white light of Kether, by now far above on the other side of the abyss. We can imagine the birds flying across that distance we ordinary humans cannot travel. The unattached wings over the mouth also symbolize the way our words take flight.

Bubbles fall down from the mouth, or rise up to the mouth from the sea underneath. Below the circle the air seems to harden into stone, again very ancient and pitted, that takes over the shape first of a wide foot, or hoof of an animal, and below that, coming out of the water, a woman on her back, reaching upwards with her head turned toward us. She is that primordial goddess of the great waters, ancient even in the Stone Age. She holds up the female pillar of the tree.

Yesod

We move to the focal point of the final triangle, Yesod, or foundation. The tree rests on this point, not Malkuth, for Malkuth receives the tree. Malkuth is the place where everything comes to rest, the seventh day of Creation, when even God called an end to labor. Yesod is the sixth day, reserved for a special moment, the creation of humans. "Male and female, God created them." Like Kether above, which contains all qualities, and

Tiferet in the middle, which balances all, Yesod, at the base, brings together the male and female pillars, with all their many variations. Yesod is imagination, and myth, and the unconscious, and in this realm, male and female do indeed mix together. Or we could say that they actually reunite, for in the unconscious we are all "divine hermaphrodites."

Imagination is the attribute of Yesod, and we might describe the creation of humans as the supreme act of divine imagination. We humans exist fully in the physical world, with all our needs and vulnerabilities and pleasures and hungers. And yet our souls reach beyond all this to perceive the divine love that fills all existence. Jewish and Christian teachings both describe humans as beyond the angels, for the angels dwell only in the spiritual realm, while humans live in both the spiritual and physical. In Christian myth, Lucifer the Light-Bringer rebelled against God when told to humble himself before Adam.

We have stressed that retelling the Bible stories does not suggest in any way that people should take the description of the six days as a literal statement of how the world and humanity came into being. We need to think Kabbalistically, that is, in metaphors that open the way to divine knowledge. The literal—the peshat, first letter of PaRaDiSe—should not control our knowledge but open the door to the other three levels. To take the literal Bible statements as reality means to live only in Malkuth, only in the narrowest physical reality, without imagination, without Yesod and all that comes above it.

This is the mistake Adam made, to take Malkuth as the sum of existence. And the story of Adam is also a metaphor, not historical fact. In Kabbalah, there is a great deal to learn and to study, even to memorize. But none of it will mean anything if we think of it on the same level as, say, a history of the Roman Empire. We need to enter the study the same way we enter the tree, through the gateway of the foundation—of imagination. We need to study Kabbalah not as simple facts but as revelations of what we might call the sacred imagination. We must become what archetypal psychologist Nor Hall calls "imaginal scholars."

"Imagination" here does not mean random flights of fancy. As the foundation, Yesod is a place of truth. The Zohar tells us that everything must return to its foundation. Everything that we think of as reality has its origin in the spiritual, and Yesod is the place of return. Henri Corbin, a philosopher and historian of Sufi traditions, created the term "imaginal" to distinguish it from "imaginary." Imaginary means whatever is not real. Imaginal means a truth revealed through our ability to perceive a reality beyond the physical.

Occult writers, especially Éliphas Lévi and Mme. Blavatsky, use the term "astral plane" to refer to this level of reality. The astral plane is a real place, as real as the room you are sitting in as you read this book. People can and do go there, and even meet there. The astral plane is Yesod, the entry to the higher levels.

If this seems a little hard to comprehend, think of this book. What does it consist of? Wood-pulp pages and ink? That is the book's existence on the physical plane. But where do the ideas exist? Do they exist in my mind, or do I create them? Do they exist in your mind as you read them? In the arrangement of the letters? If you lose this book, do the ideas vanish? Or do they exist somewhere on their own, independent of both of us? Israel Regardie calls Yesod the *anima mundi* (Latin for "world soul"), but he also uses the Jungian term *collective unconscious*.

Yesod is the place of the moon, the planetary body closest to Earth (Malkuth). In the Middle Ages and the Renaissance, people referred to ordinary existence as "sub-lunar," below the moon, for they saw the moon as the first of the spheres that surrounded Earth, and thus the gateway to higher knowledge. The moon reflects the light of the sun, and so symbolizes the imagination's ability to reflect the light of spiritual truth.

The moon governs all cycles, for it controls the tides and itself goes through birth, growth, aging, death, and rebirth every month. This is what a month originally meant, a full cycle of the moon. The menstrual cycle of human women closely follows the moon. Other mammals do not do this, and so we get a clue that human beings live on Earth, but also in heaven. We can begin to sense the higher values when we attune ourselves to the constant ebb and flow of cycles, not just in menstruation with the moon, or the tides, but the more subtle rhythms that move through life. In cycles we get glimpses of eternity.

The moon's mysterious light awakens the unconscious. It stirs in us deep connections and instinctive glimpses of deep messages. We understand, even if we cannot explain it, that we belong to something larger than our narrow lives. Because we cannot explain these intuitions intellectually, we often express them as myths, or dreams (we might describe a myth as a collective dream). The path to "higher" consciousness leads through the unconscious. If we think of the unconscious as below, or inside, normal consciousness, then to go up we must go down. This is the ancient truth of the merkavah or chariot mystics who spoke of their rise to the seven palaces (hekahloth) of heaven as the "descent" of the merkavah.

Alan Moore says that we call this sephirah Yesod, or foundation, because our spirituality is founded on imagination. And not just spirituality. To lose imagination would be a terrible thing because without it we could not envision anything at all beyond what we see narrowly in front of us. Business people could not plan new ventures, no one could fall in love, parents could not hope for a good life for their children. Imagination is the foundation of everything.

In the Haindl painting we began with the image of a bull looking down and to the right, for Haindl the side of consciousness. Here in Yesod we see a lamb look up and left, the side of the unconscious. The lamb seems to look up toward Binah, the supernal mother. Gunther Cherubini comments that Yesod is the last individual sephirah, for Malkuth is really a bringing together of all the influences, and that it is exciting to see the lamb look up, for it brings everything together. Its neck disappears into the great sea at the bottom of the tree.

Because of its mildness the lamb symbolizes the divine, especially the divine child. Christ is called the Lamb of God; Christians compare him to the lamb the Israelites sacrificed so they could mark their doors to protect themselves from the tenth plague, death. Through Yesod our animal nature turns toward the divine. Perhaps we sacrifice something of ourselves to look upwards. Sacrifice is certainly a common theme in myth and ritual in religions the world over. We cannot do this—let go or rise upwards—unless we can imagine an existence beyond the material.

Malkuth

And now we finally come to the end, to that place we think of as "the real world." Does this make it mundane, or dull, compared to all the wondrous places above? Not at all, for even though we can say that we live in Malkuth all the time, we still need to enter it—that is, become conscious that this reality, too, is part of the great mystery of the tree. Malkuth is the mystery of the physical, the world as a great spiritual wonder. If Adam mistook Malkuth for all existence it was not because he found it boring but because he found it so beautiful, so entrancing.

The Zohar tells us that the Shekhinah lives in Malkuth; that, in fact, the Shekhinah *is* Malkuth. The Shekhinah is not just the female aspect of God, as if in some sort of schematic diagram that balances male and female. The Shekhinah is God's lover, the physical world as the beloved of the Creator. And since we live in Malkuth we, too, take part in that unending love.

In the sexual imagery of the tree, sephiroth two through eight are all both feminine and masculine, for they receive energy from the sephirah above them and give it to the one below. Kether, however, is entirely masculine, for nothing exists above it but the En Sof. Malkuth is entirely feminine, for it receives from all the sephiroth above it. But this does not make it passive. Malkuth—the Shekhinah—is a feminine energy that pulses and thrills with life.

The sephiroth above Malkuth all carry qualities of eternal truths. In Malkuth time truly emerges (compared to the principle of time in Gevurah), for in Malkuth things grow, and change, and die. New things emerge, things that never existed before and never could exist without time as the great opener of possibilities. In Yesod we saw cycles, time seen as a great circle. The cycles of Yesod ebb and flow, but overall never really change. Only in Malkuth does change become possible. Malkuth is the place of evolution. From a Kabbalistic point of view the debate between science and religion, between evolution and the Bible, seems misplaced. The Creator set up this world precisely as a place of evolution, and in that great movement over time, from the Big Bang all the way through to this very moment, we can discover the living presence of the divine (the original meaning of Shekhinah).

If we think of Malkuth as time and change, it may seem paradoxical that this is the seventh day, when the great project of Creation ended and God rested. But of course paradox is the lifeblood of Kabbalah (witness all those cross-polarities), and this, too, is an aspect of Malkuth, the place where everything reveals a paradox. For what is more paradoxical than the unfolding revelation of eternity within the daily struggles and beauties of the "real world"? Or, for that matter, that the En Sof created the tree within the flash of an instant (not six twenty-four-hour days), and yet the universe has developed over many billions of years?

We will understand the idea that the Creator "rested" in Malkuth if we consider what we mean by rest. Clearly, God did not lean back, put up his/her feet on some cosmic table, and say, "Glad that's over!" So what does it mean that God/dess "ceased" from labor? Or that we should do the same? For the Creator it means that the work, the shaping of a cosmos with all its forces and energy and beauty and balance, came to a point of perfection. Not static, not rigid, because that perfection includes the evolution of existence over time. No, the image of the tree shows us a living perfection, one filled with life, as in Hermann Haindl's painting.

The idea that God rested also allows us to step back from the usual routines of our lives. Many people believe that the greatest gift of the Jews to world religion is not the Kabbalah, with all its revelations, not even the Torah, but in fact the Sabbath. Once a week, every week, we find a day that is different; a day not just to rest and restore our energies, though certainly it includes that. This is a day to look at the world in a wholly different manner, a holy manner. This is why in Jewish tradition the Sabbath takes precedence over all other sacred days. Even on the Day of Atonement, usually described as the holiest day of the Jewish year, Jews will not say certain prayers if the day happens to fall on the Sabbath.

Like all Jewish days, the Sabbath begins and ends in nature. That is, it does not begin at some arbitrary clock time, it begins when dusk falls on Friday night, and it lasts until twilight of the following day. In the sixteenth century, in the Kabbalistic town of Safed, in Galilee, the followers of Isaac Luria would dance into actual orchards (remember, *pardes* means "orchard") as the Sabbath approached. They went there not just to celebrate nature but to greet the Shekhinah, the "Sabbath bride."

The Kabbalists say that we gain an extra soul during the Sabbath. This is the *neshamah*, the spirit-soul that corresponds to the world of Beriah. And the purpose of this soul is that we might make ourselves the physical bodies of the male and female aspects of God, the Holy One, and the Shekhinah. To make love on the Sabbath will help to reunite these two sides of the divine. But why should the aspects of God need us to bring about this union? The reason is that union cannot just take place in the high abstract essences of the higher sephiroth. For a real divine union to happen it needs to happen in Malkuth. Only in Malkuth is the wholeness of Kether finally restored, for just as all the qualities separate into essences when they leave Kether, so they come back together again when the tree pours itself into Malkuth.

Many of us grew up in traditions that taught the Sabbath as a time of denial. Jews learn a long list of things they may not do. Christians learn to treat the Sabbath as grim and somber. Happily, many modern churches and synagogues have moved to a much deeper view of the day of rest, what we might call a more Kabbalistic view, that sees the Sabbath as a day of joy and wonder. We can understand the idea of an "extra" soul in a less mystical, less mythic manner. If one day a week you attempt to focus on other things than the rest of the week, if instead of work and responsibility and mindless escapism you turn yourself to spirituality and celebration, wouldn't it seem like you have a different soul on that special day?

Isabel Kliegman points out an important difference between Kabbalah and Eastern mysticism (there are many similarities). Unlike some Buddhist teachings, the Kabbalah does not consider the material world an illusion. Our souls incarnate into the world, and both the world and our bodies are very real, and very necessary. We need to take our place in Malkuth in order to learn, and challenge ourselves. Kliegman points out that Jewish tradition teaches that we live with God through prayer, study, and good works, and that all these things can only take place in Malkuth.

We can think of the nine sephiroth above Malkuth as the nine months of pregnancy. Malkuth, then, becomes the "baby," the reality that is born from the movement of energy through the stages of all the higher sephiroth. Malkuth is the densest of the sephiroth, the furthest from the pure light of Kether. But it also is the strongest, for unlike the sephiroth above it, it did not shatter when the light streamed forth from Kether. Instead, it became the resting place for the broken shards. Kliegman describes Malkuth as the place "where the work of the world gets done."

In Alan Moore's evocation of Malkuth, our world contains more than one level of reality, from the dense darkness of the underworld to the archetypal "upper" levels just this side of Yesod. I would describe the "lower" levels (again, we speak in metaphors here) as a sense of mixed energy, lumpy, where everything slides into everything else, where it's hard to tell one person's feelings or beliefs from another. When you have days in which you cannot think clearly, in which basic appetites seem to control you, in which you lash out at others or simply cannot tell where your own self stops and someone else's begins, then you have slid down to this lower level.

By contrast, in the upper levels everything appears symbolic and meaningful. We see beyond the simple facts of events or behavior to their inner truth. In this state we move toward the very edge of Malkuth, on the path that leads to Yesod. Alan Moore pictures this final path, between Yesod and Malkuth, as a highway he calls "Rt. 32" (there are twenty-two pathways but their numbers begin with eleven, because the numbers one through ten belong to the sephiroth).

We may think of this "upper" level of Malkuth as something that only mystics or poets can enter. In fact, we actually operate this way a great deal of the time. We see our actions, and other people's actions and events, as symbolic of some inner message. You may meet a man at a party and respond to him strongly, even though he's not done or said anything of great significance. If you examine your reactions you discover he reminds you of your father—and not your actual father, but a kind of image in your mind of your father. Birthdays take place in the ordinary world, but even more in these upper reaches, for what difference does one day make over another? The strong reactions we experience when we turn thirty, say, or fifty, signal that we experience such events on their symbolic level.

In the occult tradition, the body itself has layers, like concentric energy fields that radiate outwards. Beyond the physical body lies the etheric body, and beyond that the astral. These subtle bodies are like the rings of light around Malkuth in Hermann Haindl's painting.

Unlike the other sephiroth in the painting, Malkuth appears only partially, about two-thirds of it. Where the nine sephiroth above are complete and perfect, each in its own way, Malkuth—the world—is unfinished, still in a process of becoming, of discovery. Through discovery of the world around us, our consciousness allows us to discover who we are, and also to discover the spiritual reality beyond the physical.

Malkuth seems to rise out of the waters, and because of this the entire tree lifts from the bright jewel-like waves. The sea is the origin of life on our planet, and when we look at it we sense the great unknowable source of our origins. Through the tides the sea links us to Yesod, the entrance to the higher realms of the tree. The sea suggests to us the unconscious, the place of instinctual truth from which all the metaphors and images arise that bring us to spiritual understanding. The waters above are matched by the waters below and the waters below by the waters above. The Creator did not separate them and place the sky between them (day two, Gevurah) because they were different, but in order to make a space for consciousness.

The color of Malkuth is gold, a symbol of the perfection of the physical world. A rainbow radiates outwards from it, almost reaching Yesod. The colors of the rainbow are the same colors as the chakras on the human body (though only when the body is reversed, a clue to the Tarot card of the Hanged Man, and one reason why yogis stand on their heads), so that the rainbow unites heaven and Earth. Above, in Kether, we find white light, which consists of all the colors mixed together. This difference, white light in Kether and the rainbow around Malkuth, clearly shows the differences between the two sephiroth. In Kether all qualities, all colors, exist together, undifferentiated. In Malkuth they exist in their distinct forms. The interior of Malkuth is soft light, with a suggestion of human skin.

The lamb of Yesod actually rises out of Malkuth, on the right side. Our yearning for the divine moves us from ordinary consciousness to the higher awarenesses of the tree. To the right of the lamb's neck we find that vague primordial face and then the bottom of the pillar of compassion.

On the other side, the woman at the bottom of the left-hand pillar actually comes out of Malkuth. We might describe Malkuth as her womb. About the foot above her, Hermann Haindl comments that it touches her very softly, the way American Indians in their ceremonies will take great care not to tread heavily on Earth, our mother. Haindl compares this to the boots of the soldiers who conquered the Indians and their lands, and he points out that the woman smiles, as if pleased that her children touch her with such care and respect.

We do indeed walk on Earth in the sephirah of Malkuth. And the tree rises above us into the higher worlds. But it is only when we recognize our connection to Earth, to the physical, that we can open ourselves to what lies beyond. We must not mistake Malkuth for all existence. But we must not abandon it either, for everything comes into Malkuth, and it is out of Malkuth, out of our love for the world, that we begin our journeys.

EIGHT

Twenty-Two Pathways, Letters & Cards

The introduction of connecting lines on the Tree of Life adds great depth and meaning to its structure. Because there are twenty-two of them, to match the twenty-two Hebrew letters, energy in the tree does not move in just one direction. Through these pathways the tree becomes almost infinitely variable, with so many possibilities. Alan Moore, with characteristic wit, compares it to the map of the London Underground, and then calls it "an atlas of the heavens," implying yet another application of "As above, so below." Just as a map of a railroad system can show all the many ways you can make a journey, so the tree with its pathways can show you the many ways the sephiroth connect to each other. What is the difference, say, between the path that runs from Kether to Hokhmah, and the path from Kether to Binah, or the one that travels from Kether directly to Tiferet? How is the journey different in these different directions?

The pathways illuminate still more for us, because they are not just lines of connection. Each one carries its own deep meanings. This happens first of all because of their connection to the Hebrew letters. As with all ancient alphabets, the Hebrew letters do not simply indicate sounds. Instead, they represent concrete objects, such as a house for Beth

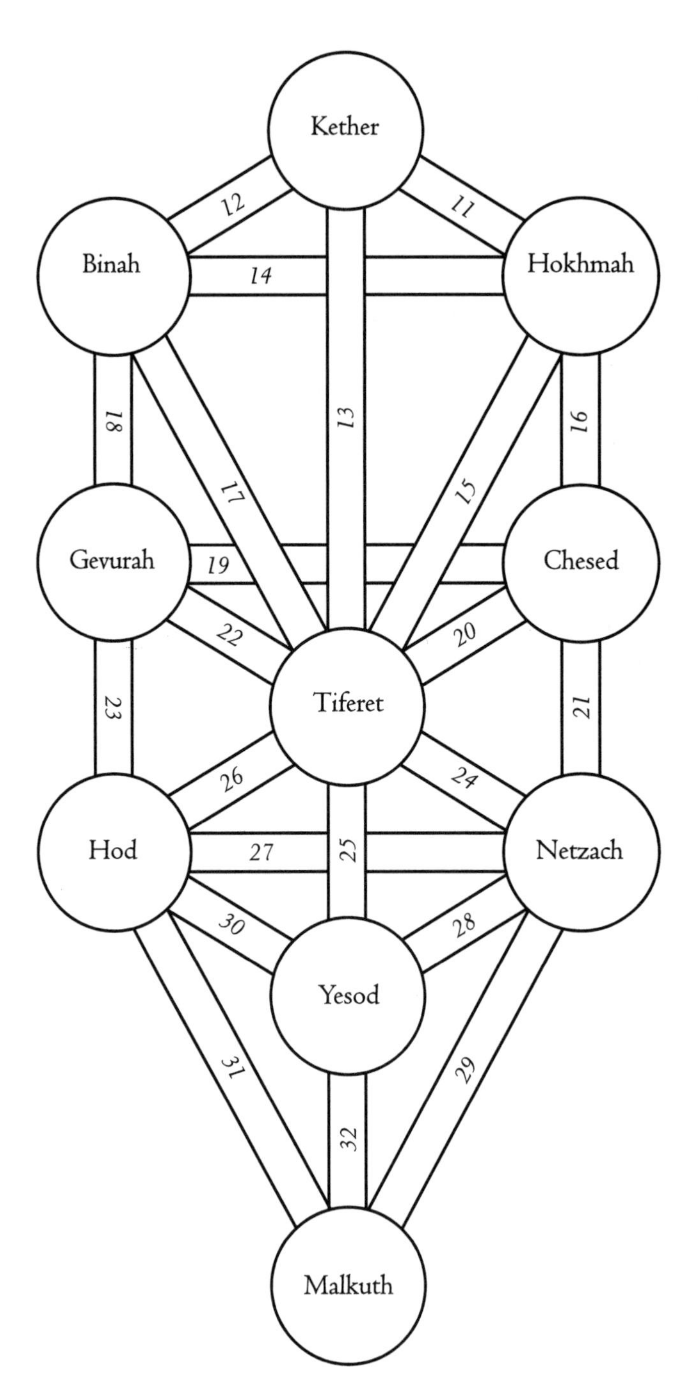

Golden Dawn Pathways on the Tree of Life

or a camel for Gimel. They also symbolize complex ideas, spiritual traditions, and emotional experiences, much like the sephiroth themselves. According to Richard Seidman, author of *The Oracle of Kabbalah*, the Hebrew word for "letter," *oht*, also means "sign," as an omen.

Because they are letters, they gain further meaning from important words where they appear. Thus the pathway from Kether to Hokhmah becomes a complex web that draws on the two sephiroth, the idea that we are moving from the undifferentiated energy of the crown to the first specific attribute, wisdom and, finally, the meanings of the letter Aleph, which include the fact that the letter makes no sound, and that it begins the first word of the Ten Commandments, God's statement of existence, "I AM."

But there is still more. In the nineteenth century the Western Kabbalah tradition introduced the idea that we can link the twenty-two trump cards of the Tarot, called the Major Arcana, to the twenty-two letters and pathways. Now we have a visual symbol as well. A good deal of the standard interpretations of these trump cards actually derive from the Kabbalistic meanings of the letters. And yet pictures carry great power, so that the imagery of the Tarot inevitably deepens our understanding of the pathways.

Though he included Hebrew letters on the cards, Hermann Haindl painted his Tarot before he ever began his interpretation of the tree. This ensures that the cards do not just illustrate a set of traditional meanings. Instead, they add to the tree all the complexity and spiritual dedication that have made the Haindl Tarot one of the most powerful decks to emerge from the literally hundreds of different Tarots published in the past quarter-century.

You can see just where all the cards go if you look closely at the painting of the tree. Each connecting line contains a Hebrew letter, and the title of the Tarot card that goes with it. In our listing here we will give the letters and cards in order, with the name of the letter spelled out, which two sephiroth it connects, the Tarot card, and a brief interpretation for each one. The number at the beginning represents the traditional Kabbalistic method of numbering the lines, beginning at eleven and continuing to thirty-two, since the numbers one through ten signify the sephiroth. In this way, we understand that the sephiroth and the pathways do not form separate systems, but one stream of energy.

Aleph, Path 11

Kether to Hokhmah. The Fool (Der Narr). Hebrew has two silent letters, Aleph and Ayin (path 25). It's possible to have a silent letter in Hebrew because only consonants are letters, so that a letter can be a carrier for vowel sounds without any sound of its own. Vowel sounds are like a breath, or a sigh, which consonants then shape, so we might get, say, Ba, or Ka (two Egyptian words for the soul). With a silent consonant we get only the breath itself, the "Aaa" of the divine as it breathes the universe into existence. For this is what happens on this first path, the very first act of Creation, as the pure energy of Kether moves into the first defined state, that of wisdom.

Aleph begins the Ten Commandments, for its silent open mouth breathes the start of the word *anokhi*, "I AM." In Jewish tradition, God gave all the detailed laws of the Torah to Moses, who then passed them on to the people, but the Ten Commandments God spoke to everyone, from within a lightning-flashed cloud on top of Mt. Sinai. In a mystical revision of this idea, some Kabbalists believe that God only spoke "aloud" the very first letter—the silent Aleph. For in truth, we can listen for the divine in the crash and thunder of existence, but perhaps even more so in silence.

Aleph also is the first letter of the word *emet* (Aleph-Mem-Tov), which means "truth." If we remove the Aleph we get only *met*, which means "death."

Aleph means "ox" or "ox-head." This is the image we find in Hermann Haindl's painting of Kether, the archaic bull worshipped as an embodiment of God's power for tens of thousands of years. We might look at the wavy lines above and below the straight line in the letter's shape as the bull's horns. Some Kabbalists see these two wavy lines as symbols of the waters "above" and "below," with the line between them as the separation that God made so that the world could exist.

Avigayil Landsman, an artist and writer on the letters, teaches that the wavy lines are each the letter Yod (path 20), the first letter in God's four-letter name. *Yod* means "hand" and she visualizes the two as God's hand reaching down to us and our hand reaching up, similar to Michelangelo's painting of the creation of man in the Sistine Chapel, where the spark of life reaches from God's finger to Adam's. She goes on to say that the line between resembles the letter Vav (path 15), the third letter in God's name, and traditionally a symbol of connections.

The Hebrew letters, remember, all carry numerical values. Aleph equals 1, the primal impulse of Creation. But Landsman points out that Yod equals 10, and Vav 6, so if we form the Aleph from two Yods and a Vav, that makes 26, which is also the sum of the four letters in God's name, Yod-Heh-Vav-Heh (10 + 5 + 6 + 5). This means that in gematria, the Kabbalist tradition of numerical interpretation of words, the letter Aleph actually equals God's most holy name.

Richard Seidman compares the shape of the letter to a ladder. Avigayil Landsman imagines it spinning about like a fan, with the two wavy lines as the blades, so that Aleph opens the whirlwind of divine energy as it brings the cosmos into being.

The Tarot card of the Fool supports these ideas, for in Tarot numbering (derived in part from the original Tarot game) the Fool equals zero, nothing. Just as we cannot pin Kether down to any specific quality, so nothing means no-thing, no limitation of any kind. And just as the line travels from the primary energy of Kether, so Tarot interpreters often describe the Fool as the great leap from cosmic nothingness into existence. This indeed is the first act of Creation, for God to choose that a universe exist at all. We should remember here that Aleph is the first letter of En Sof, the oneness of the divine beyond even Kether.

Beth (or Bet), Path 12

Kether to Binah. The Magician (Der Magier). Here we move from the unknown to what we *can* know, the sephirah of understanding. As the Great Mother, Binah represents the first sense of a solid reality. As the first letter with a sound, Beth, too, signifies the solid world that we can know and touch. Just as Aleph begins the Ten Commandments, so Beth begins the

Torah, for the first word is *Bereshith*, "In the beginning." We can think of the shape of the letter as an open mouth, and so a symbol of God speaking the universe into existence ("Let there be light"), but also human beings reading out loud the sacred texts. Beth is the first letter of Binah, the third sephirah.

Beth means "house," or "house of," as in Bethlehem, *Beth-lehem*, "house of bread," or *Beth-el*, "house of God" (the name Jacob gave to the place where he saw the vision of the ladder). A house, too, is something substantial and real. It shelters us from the raw power of nature. The letter Beth shelters us from the whirlwind of divine energy that pours forth from silent Aleph. Beth is the first letter in the Hebrew words for "blessing," and both "son" and "daughter." Certainly people think of children as a blessing, but there is a deeper meaning. A spoken blessing makes concrete and specific our general desire for good things. Children are the real result of mixing together the genetic qualities of the mother and father. So Beth represents reality.

The Tarot card of the Magician signifies creative energy, will, the power to change reality. Just as Aleph is silent and Beth has sound, so the Fool is zero and the Magician is the first actual number, one. Alan Moore describes the ultimate magical act as the creation of something out of nothing. This idea brings us right back to Beth as the first letter of Creation.

Gimel, Path 13

Kether to Tiferet. The High Priestess (Die Hohepriesterin). The final pathway out of Kether takes us down into the heart of the tree. *Gimel* means "camel," and just as a camel can cross a great desert, so the power of Gimel can sustain what is the longest journey on the tree. It is not just long but difficult, for it crosses the abyss that separates the higher and lower sephiroth. One of the words that starts with Gimel is the Hebrew for "bridge," *gesha*. This pathway is a kind of bridge between worlds, between above and below.

Gimel is very similar (same letters with only different vowel sounds) to *gamol*, a word that means "to be nourished until weaned." The energy that pours from Kether certainly is a kind of nourishment. At the same time, the arrival in Tiferet represents a sort of weaning, for the process of creation has left the pure archetypal state, the world of Emanation, and taken root in the more solid center of the tree.

There is a fascinating story in Genesis that illuminates the meaning of Gimel. Abraham has decided that his son Isaac needs a wife. He further decides that Isaac must not marry a local woman but needs someone from their homeland. However, he also declares that Isaac must not go himself, and so sends a servant with ten camels to make the journey. As soon as we encounter the number ten, we can assume we are talking of the ten sephiroth that make up existence. But what of the homeland? And why does Abraham insist that Isaac must not go there?

Suppose we make an assumption. Abraham's "homeland" is Kether, the source of all life. This is the home for all of us, but Abraham, who in Kabbalist tradition embodies Hokhmah, knows this with a wisdom beyond the rest of us. Isaac traditionally represents Chesed, first of the seven sephiroth on "our" side of the abyss. He cannot just go home again, for he belongs in the world of the seven days.

Abraham's servant travels (with the aid of all ten "camels") back to the homeland, where he meets a woman who offers water not just to him but to his animals (water in the Middle East is a precious commodity, often hoarded against outsiders). Her generosity tells the servant that he has found the right woman. He tells her and her father of his quest, and the father asks the woman, Rebecca, if she will travel to Isaac and marry him. Now, in that time and place young women ordinarily did not get to agree or disagree about marriage. Rebecca, however, symbolizes the soul that must travel from the world of pure existence to the physical world, and nothing can force this journey. For a soul to journey across the abyss into the physical is the essence of free will.

Rebecca makes the journey riding on a camel. From a distance, Genesis tells us, she sees Isaac and is so stricken with his beauty that she falls off her camel. This is indeed the "fall," from pure spirit into physical existence. But it is a willing fall, a desire fulfilled. The two marry and become lovers. Since Rebecca will now embody Gevurah, their union takes place in Tiferet. This is the journey that Rebecca makes on her camel, down that long path of Gimel, from Kether to Tiferet. Isaac and Rebecca "know" each other as sexual beings, for remember that the gimel path travels through the sexual mysteries of Da'ath, that hidden sephirah that dwells in the abyss.

It is not just desire that makes this journey possible. Remember that Rebecca showed her perfection through her concern for the animals. The letter Gimel begins an important phrase in Hebrew, *gimalut chasidim*, acts of loving-kindness. These are said to be one of the pillars that uphold the world. When the energy moves from Kether to Tiferet, that is a kind of loving act, for without that divine energy the physical world would be lifeless and empty. But the path goes two ways, and we can say that our own acts of loving-kindness—generosity, charity, compassion—carry us on our own journeys to our spiritual "homeland."

The Tarot card for Gimel is the High Priestess. In Hermann Haindl's version of this card a camel crouches in front of the priestess, whose eyes open wide in wonder. This card represents "secret" teachings—not in the sense of something concealed from outsiders but, rather, perceptions and awarenesses so deep we cannot put them into words. We identify this card with the sea, vast and deep and mysterious, the sea as an image of the great depths of spiritual truth. If we can make that journey from Tiferet up to Kether, we will learn the High Priestess's secrets.

Daleth, Path 14

Hokhmah to Binah. The Empress (Die Herrscherin). This pathway completes the upper triangle of the tree. At the same time, it is the first path that does not originate in Kether, but instead crosses between the right and left pillars. We can think of it as the marriage line of the primal masculine Hokhmah and the primal feminine Binah. The Tarot card of the Empress represents passion, a fitting card for this union.

The Hebrew letter for this path, Daleth, means "door," as if it opens between the two parts of the tree. The bent-over shape of the letter suggests humility, a word that, like human, comes from the Latin *humus*, which means "dirt." This is the same idea as Hebrew, for the name of the first human, Adam, means "red dirt." These connections fit very well with Hermann Haindl's work, where people bend over, not in submission to some authority, but as a way to return to our mother, the earth. The earth as mother is one of the themes of both the sephirah Binah and the Tarot card of the Empress.

Heh, Path 15

Hokhmah to Tiferet. The Emperor (Der Herscherr). This is the first line from the right side to the center of the tree. Except for Malkuth, every sephirah connects to Tiferet. Like path 13, this line also crosses the abyss, though it does not travel through Da'ath or make as long a journey. It takes the power of wisdom and brings it to the center, to contribute to that idea of Tiferet as the perfect being.

Heh means "behold" and, by extension, the idea of a window, something we look through. From Tiferet we can look (back) through this letter to behold the wonders of wisdom.

Heh is the second and fourth letter of God's most holy name, Yod-Heh-Vav-Heh. This is the female letter, another example of cross-polarity since the line originates in the primal male sephirah. The Bible actually gives us many names for God. Some readers will recognize one of them, Yah, from the word *hallelujah*, which means "praise Yah." *Yah* is spelled Yod-Heh. Yod symbolizes heaven or the world to come, and Heh this world, the reality we know. Together they make up Creation.

When Moses encounters the burning bush and hears God speaking to him, he answers with a word of commitment that begins with Heh: *hineini*, which means "here I am." God tells him to take off his shoes, for he stands on holy ground. Holy ground exists anywhere we are willing to give ourselves to God and say "here I am."

The Tarot card is the Emperor, a card of structures and laws and the ability of humans to comprehend God's plan. This indeed is wisdom brought to beauty, Hokhmah to Tiferet. The Emperor can become arrogant if we start to believe that our intellect separates us from the earth.

When he discussed this card from his Tarot deck, Hermann Haindl said, "The Empress creates the Emperor."

Vav, Path 16

Hokhmah to Chesed. The Hierophant (Der Hierophant). This is the first path to run entirely down the right-hand, masculine pillar. The right-hand pillar represents the expansive open quality of compassion, and so the line moves from wisdom to mercy. It reminds us that mercy is not foolish, or indulgent, or a denial of reality—all arguments we often encounter—but in fact the way of divine wisdom.

The Hebrew letter is Vav, the third letter of Yod-Heh-Vav-Heh. As we can see from the shape, *Vav* means "hook," or "nail." This makes it a letter of connections. The Tarot card of the Hierophant represents traditional teachings, including Kabbalah itself, for these teachings connect us both to generations past and to the wisdom discovered long ago. In the sacred name, Vav stands between the two Hehs, the two feminine letters that we might think of as the waters above and the waters below. Vav connects them and at the same time represents that separation that makes it possible for the world to exist.

Zayin, Path 17

Binah to Tiferet. The Lovers (Die Liebenden). Zayin moves from the supernal mother, Binah, to the center, supplying Tiferet with all the strength and devotion of the feminine and the power of the pillar of judgment. *Zayin* means "a weapon"; Western Kabbalah more specifically describes it as a "sword." To wield a weapon decisively and for good is a quality of the left-hand pillar.

Western Kabbalah sees the sword as a mental weapon, for a sharp mind can cut through illusions. It separates and discriminates between one thing and another. The Tarot card of the Lovers might seem an odd match with a sword or weapon. Early versions of this card, however (in particular the Tarot de Marseille, usually thought of as the standard, or classical, Tarot), show a young man choosing between two women. The idea of choice clearly belongs to the discriminatory power of the left-hand pillar and the image of the sword.

As the seventh letter, Zayin suggests the seven days of Creation and their completion on the Sabbath. Sabbath is a time of peace, and the left-hand pillar teaches us to use swords and other weapons as tools to bring peace. In relation to the card of the Lovers, we can remember that the Sabbath does not simply celebrate the soul, but body and soul. Comfort, good food, beautiful clothes, and indeed sexual love, all belong to the celebration of the seventh day.

Chet, Path 18

Binah to Gevurah. The Chariot (Der Wagen). This is the first path entirely on the left side, moving from the great mother to the daughter, from Sarah to Rebecca (compare this to the right side, with the move from father to son, Abraham to Isaac). This is the final path that crosses the abyss from the upper triangle to the lower seven. Mythologically we might visualize this as a generational change, from the primal forces to those more accessible to human understanding.

Chet means "fence" or "enclosure." This suggests a kind of safe zone for human consciousness as we descend from the higher to the lower letters.

Though Chet appears on the left, it actually forms the first letter of Chesed, reminding us once again that the attributes of right and left are not strictly separate but constantly move in and out of each other. Chet also begins the Hebrew word *chai*, or "life," spelled Chet-Yod. Chet has the shape of an archway or shelter, while Yod is the first letter of the great name. Yod symbolizes the divine spark, and so we can say that life comes when that spark enters a physical form.

The Tarot card is the Chariot, an image of will and movement. The strong energy of the Chariot evokes the movement into Gevurah, the sephirah of power. In Hermann Haindl's version of this card, a kind of raw energy moves behind the Chariot, propelling it forward.

Tet, Path 19

Chesed to Gevurah. Strength (Die Kraft). This is the second of three crossing lines that connect the right and left pillars. Here we join the son and daughter, Chesed and Gevurah. *Tet* means "snake," a creature who symbolically joins male and female, for its basically phallic form can curl around itself to resemble the folds of the vulva. As the ninth letter it suggests the nine months (nine lunar periods) of pregnancy. At the same time, we find it in the words for "rod" and "staff," recalling both Moses parting the Sea of Reeds (not the Red Sea, as commonly believed) and the famous Twenty-Third Psalm, "Thy rod and thy staff, they comfort me."

Richard Seidman points out an interesting parallel in the Greek image of the caduceus. Created by the god Hermes (who gives his name to the Western Hermetic Tradition), the caduceus is a staff wound around with two snakes. Invested with the power to heal (a present-day symbol of the medical profession), the caduceus brings together male and female. It also represents the kundalini serpent energy that winds around the spine in two streams.

Hermann Haindl's version of the Strength card evokes the image of kundalini energy uncoiled, for it shows a woman shaman holding a snake above her head.

Yod, Path 20

Netzach to Tiferet. The Hermit (Der Eremit). This line takes the energy of Netzach into the center of the tree, Tiferet. Yod is the first letter of God's name, that spark of creative energy. Its small size, like a flash of light, can remind us of the Big Bang, or the moment that light emerged from the En Sof. Yod is the only letter suspended in mid-air (if we drew a line under all the letters, only Yod would not touch it), as if at the moment of

Creation. *Yod* means "hand," the hand of Yah, or Yod-Heh-Vav-Heh, as it reaches down to begin life. As the tenth letter it represents the ten fingers that we ourselves use to build or write or draw, any of the actions that make our human culture.

The Tarot card is the Hermit, a figure who steps back from the ordinary world to look deeply into the mysteries of existence. He often holds up a lantern, using wisdom to light the way for others. In Hermann Haindl's version he stands among animals and looks up joyously at a light above him.

Kaph, Path 21

Chesed to Netzach. The Wheel of Fortune (Der Schickselrad). This line completes the right-hand pillar of the tree that runs from Hokhmah to Chesed to Netzach, from the high and distant wisdom to mercy to the inner truth and victory of eternity. The letter Kaph actually ties the whole tree together; it begins the word Kether (crown), the top sephirah, and appears in Malkuth (kingdom), the final sephirah. Kaph also begins the word *kisay*, or "throne." All these royal terms suggest an inner majesty of spirit. Kaph also begins an important word in Kabbalah, *kavannah*, which means "concentration" and refers to the intensity of focus that allows spiritual exercises (such as contemplation of the tree, or meditative travel along its pathways) to produce truly transcendent states.

Literally, *Kaph* means "the palm of the hand." This suggests productive labor. If we connect this idea to all those royal words, we get the idea of work that ennobles us and makes us the equal of kings. The Tarot card for this path is the Wheel of Fortune, an image that symbolizes karma, or the wheel of life, that turns and turns and always brings change. The palm of the hand, however, hints that we can seize the center of the wheel rather than allow ourselves to spin 'round and 'round on the rim. We do this through the kavannah of spiritual awareness.

Lamed, Path 22

Gevurah to Tiferet. Justice (Die Gerechtigkeit). We switch sides now and bring the power of Gevurah to the center. *Lamed* means "goad" and in particular an ox-goad, as if we use the power of Gevurah to goad that Aleph ox, the silent letter, into a more tangible physical existence in the heart of the tree. Lamed begins the Hebrew words for both "learn" and "teach," and so encompasses the most Kabbalist of activities, study. Kabbalah has never been a path of pure sensation, but always has used study to *goad* us into higher consciousness. Lamed, alone of the Hebrew alphabet, reaches above the height of all the other letters. Through learning we extend ourselves above ordinary awareness.

This is not learning for its own sake, in which we believe we accomplish something just by memorizing a great deal of information. We need to learn with that spiritual kavannah we looked at in the previous letter. We will understand this better when we know that Lamed also begins the Hebrew word for "heart," *lev*. We spell this word Lamed-Vav. The numerical value of lev is thirty-six (after the tenth letter, the number values jump to produce higher numbers; Lamed equals thirty, and Vav equals six). A Jewish legend tells of thirty-six "just men" who secretly uphold the world through their compassion. Thirty-six is eighteen times two, and eighteen is the numerical value of *chai*, the word for "life," and the name of the transcendent soul of Atzilut, the first world.

The Tarot card is Justice. This is a card of truth and honesty, and also of emotion, for it is spiritual justice, and spiritual justice demands that we open the heart. Hermann Haindl's painting for this card emphasizes the perfectly balanced scales, an image that goes back to ancient Greece, and before that to Egypt. In the Egyptian Book of the Dead we learn that after a person died the goddess Ma'at and the god Thoth (the mythical creator of the Tarot, and the same as Hermes Trismegistus) weighed the person's heart against an ostrich feather. An ostrich feather weighs almost nothing. Symbolically, this myth tells us that we must open the heart and release all guilt and fear if we want to experience a spiritual rebirth.

Mem, Path 23

Gevurah to Hod. The Hanged Man (Der Gehangte). This path matches the previous one on the other side of the tree. It completes the left-hand pillar that goes from Binah to Gevurah to Hod. The letter Mem is the second of the three mother letters identified in the Sefer Yetsirah. Just as Aleph symbolized the element of air, so Mem represents water. The actual Hebrew word for "water," *mayim*, in fact consists of two Mems with a Yod between them. Once again, we might think of the upper and lower waters, this time with the Yod as the divine creative spark that separates them.

Gevurah and Hod are both on the female left pillar, and Mem appears in several feminine words, usually as the last letter. "Mother" in Hebrew is *ahm*, "womb" is *racham*. The sea, so often identified with women and the womb, is *yam* (or *yahm*). This last word forms the second syllable of the name Miryam, the name of Moses's sister and the original Hebrew name of Mary, the mother of Jesus.

The Hanged Man is a card of surrender. We reverse our previous values and give ourselves to the spiritual path. For Hermann Haindl this means the feminine power of the earth. His Hanged Man is ecstatic rather than pained. A rainbow appears across his body, while the land beneath him takes on the shape of a pregnant woman.

Nun, Path 24

Tiferet to Netzach. Death (Der Tod). This is the first of three paths leading out of Tiferet to the lower part of the tree. Previously, paths went into Tiferet and so contributed to its perfect balance. Here Tiferet gives out energy, imbuing the sephirah of eternity with the beauty of the tree's central sephirah. Of course, as always in the tree, the path goes in both directions. If we imagine ourselves traveling up the tree to Kether, then one of the possible routes takes us from Netzach to Tiferet.

The letter *Nun* means "fish," a creature that swims in the waters of the previous letter. Just as Mem represented Mary, so the fish, for Christians, symbolizes Christ. Partly this has to do with the idea that every two thousand years constitutes an astrological "age," and the birth of Jesus began the age of Pisces, the sign of the fish. It also comes from a more general symbolism of the fish as the soul, because it swims in the deep waters of the earth's womb, the sea. Fish also make good fertilizers for the soil. As well as a fish, Nun also means "to sprout, to grow." When the Wampanoag Indians taught the New England Pilgrims to bury a fish in the dirt with their seeds they were unknowingly linking the Pilgrims to their biblical roots. The Tree of Life grows in all cultures.

In Hebrew numbering Nun equals fifty. Richard Seidman writes that there are fifty gates of spiritual understanding. Forty-nine of them (seven times seven) lead us to states within our ordinary lives. The fiftieth, however, takes us beyond our "current plane of existence."

In connection with the theme of rebirth and transcendence of the physical, the Tarot card here is Death. Though movies love to show the Death card as a prediction of something terrible, such as murder, the picture has always symbolized a passage, and the letting go of old things.

Samekh, Path 25

Tiferet to Yesod. Alchemy (traditionally Temperance) (Die Alchemie). This is the second of three pathways that travel from Tiferet to the lower triangle, this time to the base of the triangle. This path, therefore, moves us from the center to the foundation, from perfect balance to the deep power of the imagination. It also moves from the sun to the moon, from direct light to reflection.

Samekh means "a support" or "a prop." Many Kabbalists describe it as a tent peg. Since the ancient Hebrews lived in tents for centuries before they ever built cities, a tent peg was indeed a vital support for human existence. Tradition describes Cain, the first murderer, as also the inventor of cities, an attitude we still find in the modern world, where many people consider cities decadent and removed from humans' natural state.

The form of Samekh is unbroken, without gaps, and therefore without end or beginning. This gives it a quality of eternity, like the famous image of a snake biting its own tail. Many significant Hebrew words begin with Samekh. These include *sukkah*, a sacred hut; *sefer*, a book (as in the Sefer Yetsirah); *siddur*, a prayerbook; and *sipur*, a story. Most significant for our purposes, Samekh begins both *sephirah*, the basis of the tree itself, and *sod,* the word for "secret." Sod, remember, is the last aspect of PaRDeS, or Paradise, the secret, or mystical, meaning of a text or symbol.

The Tarot card is called Alchemy in the Haindl Tarot, Temperance in traditional decks. As the card after Death, it indicates a transcendence of limitations. The Haindl image emphasizes the union of life and death, male and female, with energies that flow back and forth between these seeming opposites. This kind of blended polarities is one of the secrets (sod) of Kabbalah, which sets up a seeming duality only to constantly cross energies back and forth.

Ayin, Path 26

Tiferet to Hod. The Devil (Der Teufel). This is the third and final line out of Tiferet. Where path 24 moved the energy to the love and emotion of Netzach, here it shifts from the balance of the center to the strong mind energy of Hod. Hod, remember, is the sephirah of Mercury, also identified with Hermes and Thoth.

The letter is Ayin, which means "eye." Ayin is the second silent letter, along with Aleph. This is partly paradoxical (like so much of Kabbalah), for one of the attributes of Hod is language. And yet we know that we can reach a state of mystic awareness where the "eye"—inner vision—can gaze upon wonders we cannot really put into words. And of course, until the invention of Braille, the written aspect of language has always depended on the eye.

Because of the dominance of sight among the senses, the eye has a special place in spiritual symbolism. The Egyptians spoke of the "eye of Horus" as the center of the god's power. We speak of prophets as "seers," and the psychic center in the brain as the "third eye." And yet we also fear the "evil eye" (the Hebrew phrase is *ayin hora*), the power to curse someone with a look of hate or envy. The eye is one way we communicate with God. Richard Seidman quotes the Christian mystic Meister Eckhart: "My eye and God's eye" seeing one another are "one eye." Isaiah speaks of seeing God "eye to eye" (52:8).

And yet the eye can also fool us. We all witness an optical illusion every single day of our lives, when we watch the sun rise up out of the east, travel across the sky, and disappear into the west. The sun, of course, doesn't go anywhere; the Earth turns on its axis.

The most serious illusion is materialism, the doctrine that tells us nothing exists except what we can see and measure. Despite all the testimony of mystics and shamans and visionaries and seers through all the millennia, materialists will insist it is all superstitious nonsense if they themselves cannot see it. This is one reason the Tarot card here is the Devil, for the Devil is the master of illusion. Among the chief illusions is the idea that a supernatural ruler of damned souls actually exists, and can separate us from God. Kabbalah teaches that nothing can separate us from God, because we never leave God. We just need to open our eyes. Hermann Haindl has painted the central figure in this card as a goat with a jewel in the place of the third eye. For a new edition he also changed the title to Pan, a Greek god of sensuality and ecstatic play.

Peh, Path 27

Netzach to Hod. The Tower (Der Turm). This is the final line uniting the two pillars. Here the line runs from the overflowing emotion of Netzach to the brilliance of Hod, from the eternity and victory of love to the glory and splendor of intellect. This makes it one of the most powerful pathways on the tree, and we shall see in a moment that the Tarot card for twenty-seven, the Tower, symbolizes explosions of energy and revelation.

Peh means "mouth," and so symbolizes the faculty of speech. We communicate both ideas and emotions through speech. In speech we declare ourselves, state our beliefs and values. For Moses to commit himself to the divine path he had to say, out loud, "Hineini" ("Here I am"). With

Ayin we quoted Isaiah's promise to see God "eye to eye"; here we can cite the statement in Numbers (12:8) that Moses spoke with God "mouth to mouth." Richard Seidman points out that the Buddhists consider Right Speech part of the eightfold path to enlightenment, and that Jesus tells his followers (Matt. 15:11) "Not that which goes into the mouth defiles a person; but that which comes out of the mouth, this defiles a person." Christians believe that the chain of sin from Adam finally ends when Christ calls out on the cross "It is finished!"

The card of the Tower shows a tower struck by lightning and on fire. People often take it to mean the destruction of false values, but it is far more than that. It symbolizes what I call "God speech," or revelation. The lightning is that very enlightenment the Buddha experienced, the flash that transformed St. Paul on the way to Damascus, the lightning flash of Creation that descends from Kether to Malkuth in less than an instant.

Genesis tells of the Tower of Babel (possibly inspired by the ziggurats of Babylon, worked on by people of many lands). Because the people tried to build a material construction that would reach heaven, the Creator scrambled their speech. Later, God speaks to humanity at Mt. Sinai out of thunder and lightning. And in the Christian New Testament, Pentecost celebrates a kind of anti-Babel when the Holy Spirit enters people and they "speak in tongues" and each one understands the other. When contemporary Pentecostal Christians speak "in tongues" it often sounds like "babble" to outsiders. Shamans, however, do the same thing, speak in a divine language no one else understands, while Hasidic Jews often chant in wordless melodies to express their devotion to God. All these forms of ecstatic "speech" belong to path 27.

Tzadi, Path 28

Netzach to Yesod. The Star (Der Stern). Here we move from the right-hand side, the sephirah of love, to the base of the triangle, the foundation of imagination—Venus to the moon. *Tzadi* means "fish hook," as if we dip into the great sea of the unconscious and bring forth images, flashes, emotions. If we remember that Nun means fish, and rebirth of the soul, then fish hook suggests whatever brings our soul forth into higher consciousness.

Tzadi is the first letter in two important sacred words. The first is *tzaddik* (holy person), a title similar to the Catholic term "saint," though not as formal (no process exists to officially declare someone a tzaddik). Related to tzaddik is *tzedakkah*, or "charity," for the primary characteristic of a tzaddik is a person of great charity and compassion.

The Tarot card here is the Star, a card of great importance in the Haindl Tarot. Traditionally, the Star shows a nude woman freely pouring water from two gourds onto the earth. It symbolizes the freedom and openness that come after the upheaval of the Tower, what we might call the calm after the storm. In the Haindl Tarot it also represents the hope of renewal for the earth. The picture shows a woman, dressed very simply, who bends over to cleanse herself in a rocky stream. She represents Gaia, the Greek goddess of the earth, and the name of a scientific concept that describes the entire planet as a single living organism. Despite all the dangers we ourselves have created for the earth, the Star promises hope and belief in the future.

Koof, Path 29

Netzach to Malkuth. The Moon (Der Mond). We stay on the right side of the tree, where we make the first of three connections to Malkuth, the "real world." This path establishes the connection of love to daily life. Through love we can reach beyond ordinary consciousness to sense the bottom of the right-hand pillar of mercy. Kabbalists link Koof with the back of the head, which is to say the instinctive part of the brain. This is not simply metaphor. The base of the brain, which rests in the back of the skull, contains areas similar to the brains of lizards, who after all are the descendants of the dinosaurs. This part of the brain, therefore, is far older than humanity itself. Compare Koof to the following letter, Resh, which means "head" and signifies the cortex.

Koof begins a number of important words, most notably Kabbalah itself. Other words include *kadosh*, holy; *kedushah*, holiness; and *kaddish*, a prayer in praise of God. The last word refers to a specific prayer recited in various situations, but most famously as part of mourning a dead relative. Jews who say kaddish for a parent or spouse are often surprised to discover the prayer says nothing about death but only praises God as a giver of life. This is our deepest instinct, that life fills all existence.

The Tarot card of the Moon also evokes our instincts. Dogs will howl at the moon, and police and hospitals often report increased emergencies and bizarre behavior under a full moon. (I have read that statistically there is no actual increase, but clearly it *feels* that way to the police and hospital personnel.) The reflected light of the moon seems to touch all the way to that back of the skull to release something very ancient in us, a reminder of everything beyond the safety of our rational human culture.

Resh, Path 30

Hod to Yesod. The Sun (Die Sonne). We move to the left side of the tree now, for the last two paths that will come from the pillar of judgment. Thirty takes us from the intellect of Hod into the imagination of Yesod, a journey into the unconscious. In one of those paradoxes that occur so often in the tree, the letter for this path means "head," and signifies consciousness. It represents in particular the front of the head and the cerebral cortex, the part of the brain that makes us distinctly human. We might say that it is just when we enter the dark unconscious that we need to retain the light of awareness.

Resh begins several important words, such as *racham*, womb, and *rachamim*, compassion. It begins *rav*, rabbi, which means "teacher," and it begins *rasha*, to do wrong. These are qualities of free will, to be compassionate and wise or to be selfish and hurtful. We could not experience such choices without the consciousness that comes in the cortex. Many people will know resh in the form of *rosh*, for Rosh Hashanah, the Jewish New Year, literally the head of the year. This day, mythologically seen as the anniversary of Creation, begins a time of both heightened consciousness and introspection known as the Days of Awe, the ten days leading up to the Day of Atonement. Again, it is consciousness that allows us to acknowledge our desire to become at one ("at-onement") with the divine. This desire is the basis, the Yesod, of the entire tree; not knowledge, or power, or magic, but oneness with the infinite oneness of God and our own divine selves.

The Tarot card here is the Sun, an image of radiant light. The sun signifies higher consciousness in many cultures. The ancient Egyptians looked upon the sun as the supreme god Ra; Native Americans speak of Grandfather Sun; medieval Christians saw the sun as the light of Christ. Hermann Haindl's image of the Sun card is otherworldly, mysterious; not just the burning ball of hydrogen that dominates the day sky, but the solar light of divine consciousness.

Shin, Path 31

Hod to Malkuth. Aeon/Judgement (Das Aeon). The next to last path travels from the bottom of the left pillar into the "real" world of Malkuth. We are leaving the artificial separation into abstract principles and returning to wholeness, for Malkuth is the only sephirah other than Kether that contains all qualities. Kether gave them forth, separating the tree into polarities, and now Malkuth receives them all, restoring totality even if the "denseness" of Malkuth, its everyday reality, obscures this great truth. The tree reminds us that all the qualities of "above" appear together here in the "below" of our own lives.

The shape of Shin appears like a flame with three tongues, and indeed Shin is the final of the three mother letters, the element of fire. The word for "fire" is *esh*, Aleph-Shin, the mother letter for air and the mother letter for fire. The third of the mothers comes in when we find that the word for "heaven" is *shamayim*, the word for water plus the letter Shin.

Shin is a remarkably positive letter. It begins the words *shalom*, peace; *Shaddai*, the name of God derived from "breasts" and usually translated as Almighty; *shanah*, year, derived from *shinah*, change; and *simcha*, joy or joyous event. It also starts two words very important to Kabbalah, *Shabbat* and *Shekhinah*. Both these words return us to Malkuth, for the final sephirah symbolizes the Sabbath and becomes the dwelling place of the Shekhinah.

The Tarot card here is called Aeon in the Haindl Tarot, a name Haindl borrowed from Aleister Crowley. The traditional card is called Judgement, and shows the Christian myth of the angel whose trumpet raises the dead for the Last Judgement. The secret of this card has always been that unlike the actual Christian concept no one is actually "judged," that is, condemned to hell. Instead, everyone rises up joyously so that the card means the emergence of higher consciousness, in which we are both the resurrected souls and the angel who sounds the music of new life.

The switch to Aeon introduces the idea of a great epochal shift in the world, a rebirth not just for individuals but for all existence. This is a time of great danger and fear, but also of great hope, symbolized in the picture by a fetus that floats down to Earth. Hermann Haindl suggests we view our great crises as the signal of such an epochal change.

Tav, Path 32

Yesod to Malkuth. The Universe/World (Das Universum). Finally we come to the end of the journey, what Alan Moore calls "Rt. 32," where the foundation of the tree pours down into the reality we know, or think we know. Moore calls this path between Yesod and Malkuth "flesh and imagination's dance" (*Promethea*, issue 12).

Malkuth is "kingdom," and we might think of it as the earthly kingdom of physical existence. And yet it also is what Jesus called "the Kingdom of Heaven," for Kabbalah teaches us that heaven does not lie somewhere far across the sky or after death, but within ourselves, within every breath, every drop of water, every leaf and pebble. This is indeed the great secret, the sod, of PRDS, PaRaDiSe.

The letter Tav means a mark, or a seal. We might say that this last letter and path puts the seal on our journey of the tree. According to Richard Seidman, Kabbalah tradition tells us that the alphabet does not end in Tav but begins again with Aleph, as if the whole alphabet, all the pathways of the tree, form a great circle. In the Sefer Yetsirah we read, "The end is embedded in the beginning and the beginning in the end." Remember that if we take all three mother letters, Aleph-Mem-Tav, we get the word *emet*, "truth." But if we leave out the silent Aleph, the beginning, if we do not see the spirit within the physical, then we get only *met*, "death."

Tav begins some of the most sacred words in Hebrew, such as Torah, Talmud, and Tanakh (the Hebrew title for the Bible). It also begins *teshuvah*, "repentance," literally a turning toward God, and the Isaac Luria teaching of *tikkun*, for "restore," as in *tikkun olam*, "restore the world."

The traditional name for the last Tarot trump card is the World, but Aleister Crowley renamed it Universe, making it clear that we do not limit our vision to what we might call "this world," that is, the world of our senses. In Hermann Haindl's version, the Norse Midgard serpent awakens to breathe the fire of new life, an image both of teshuvah and tikkun. His Tarot card shows the bottom half of the earth, while his painting of the tree shows the top half of Malkuth. The two actually form one great vision, what we might call "paint and imagination's dance," for in fact, every work of art re-creates that sacred pathway between Yesod and Malkuth. In the deepest way, Hermann Haindl's art reminds us that we cannot just study Kabbalah, we must live it, with commitment and love.

APPENDIX

Readings *on the* Tree of Life

There are several ways we can use Tarot with the tree. For all of these, Hermann Haindl's painting aids our work or study, for we can set the cards on the painting itself and as a result bring our readings more vividly to life. The first thing we can do with the cards is lay them out in their places on the tree. If we actually place the Fool on the line between Kether and Hokhmah, the Magician between Kether and Binah, and so on, we can get a deeper sense of how everything fits together. The images will feel more three dimensional, more alive, as we ourselves take the step to bring the two great symbolic systems in line with each other.

You also can use Tarot cards to illuminate the four worlds. Using first one suit then another, place cards one through ten on the sephiroth. In other words, take the suit of Wands, place the ace on Kether, the two on Hokhmah, and so on until you place the ten on Malkuth. Repeat this for all four suits and see both how the cards change your sense of the tree, and the tree images—the snakes at Chesed and Gevurah, for example, or the birds at Tiferet, Netzach, and Hod—change your perceptions of the cards.

You also can set the court cards on the tree. Here we can use all four suits at once (there are only four per suit). We will use the Haindl designations, with traditional names in parentheses. The attributions and places on the tree come from the connection of the four court cards to

God's four-letter name, and the four elements. The Fathers (Kings) symbolize the first letter Yod, and fire. Try setting them across the sephirah of Hokhmah. The Mothers (Queens) represent Heh, and water. They go on Binah. The Sons (Knights) signify Vav, and air. Set them down at Tiferet. Finally, the Daughter cards (Pages) represent the second Heh, and earth. They go at Malkuth. (Readers who have learned the Aleister Crowley cards need to know that the names on the cards are different than the tradition. The sequence goes Knight-Queen-Prince-Princess.)

Setting the cards on the tree in these ways helps us to understand the tree better. It also gives greater insight into the cards, for it places them within the large and complex system that actually lies behind much of their symbolism. For example, people who have worked with the cards probably will have noticed that the five in each suit usually shows some sort of harsh scene or difficulty. The reason for this becomes clearer when we know that five is the sephirah Gevurah, and that Gevurah expresses the power to take on life's tougher challenges.

But we do not have to use the cards only in their appointed places. Instead, we can do readings directly on the tree. A Tarot reading that uses a preset pattern is called a "spread," and the tree makes a particularly dynamic spread pattern.

Set the painting before you (you don't need to use it, but it will make the reading far more vivid). Shuffle the cards in whatever manner works best for you (just make sure to keep the cards picture-side down so you do not see what they are). Then, one by one, set them down in the pattern of the sephiroth, until you have a card for each sephirah.

From the symbolic meanings we have seen, it is obvious that each sephirah invites many possible interpretations, so we need to make some choices to come up with meanings that will work in a Tarot spread. The following meanings differ slightly from an earlier version I developed for my book *Seventy-Eight Degrees of Wisdom*. They reflect the understanding I hope I have gained through working on this book. Readers also might want to take a look at the meanings developed by other interpreters, especially Isabel Kliegman in her book *Tarot and the Tree of Life*.

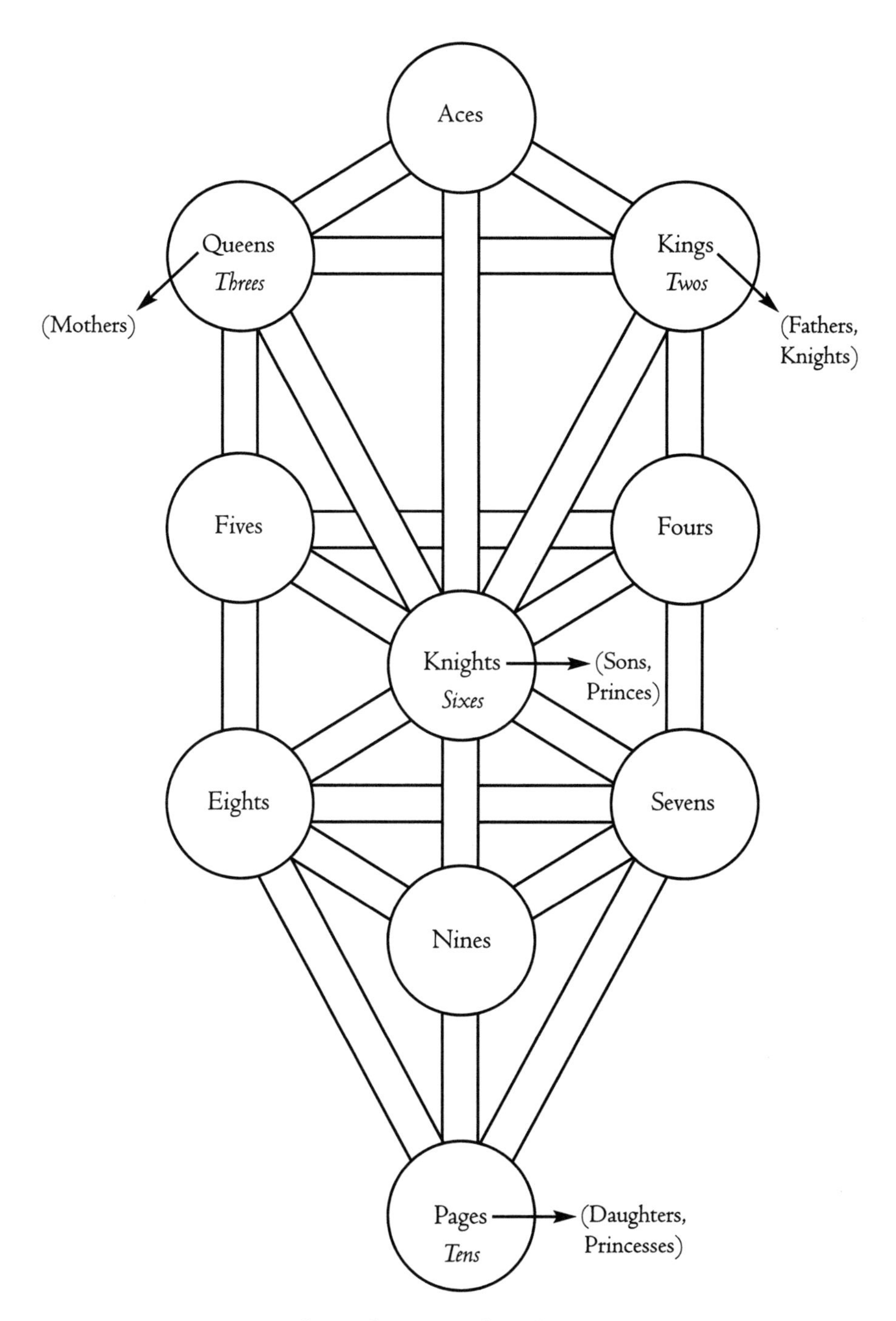

Numbers and Court Cards on the Tree of Life

Kether—The highest potential for a person or a situation. What is possible. The spiritual truth in a situation.

Hokhmah—Wisdom. What we have learned, or can learn. Whatever aids us in realizing the highest potential shown in Kether.

Binah—How we can apply what we have learned. Facing life's difficulties and challenges. What holds us back from our highest potential and how we can turn that around to gain deeper understanding.

Chesed—What we give to other people, emotionally and practically. The part of us that is most open and generous and loving. Ways in which we show mercy and compassion for those around us who are suffering.

Gevurah—How we have and express power. Ways to be strong, to set boundaries. The best approach to take when encountering some opposition or painful situation.

Tiferet—How we find or express beauty and joy in life, in relationships, in family, in our work. Ways in which we balance the many aspects of our lives. The center of who we are.

Netzach—Emotions, love, how we express our emotions. The importance of love and feelings in a situation or a person's life.

Hod—Intellect, how a person's mind works. The things we need to think about and analyze. Language, the ways we express ourselves.

Yesod—Imagination, the unconscious, dreams. The images and fantasies we have in our imagination, how they affect our lives, and what comes from them. A chance to look at the foundation of who we really are.

Malkuth—Outer circumstances and conditions. How these things affect us. The issues a person must face, in life or a situation.

Da'ath—Hidden knowledge, knowledge that transforms.

Since Da'ath is transformation, I prefer to do it last. Others, however, may choose to set it down between the cards for Binah and Chesed. You can do this reading as a way to look at a person's life pattern overall, or for a specific time or situation.

It also is possible to do a Tree of Life reading using the entire deck. To do this, you first need to remove one card (I am going to describe this as a reading you do for yourself, but you easily can use the methods for someone else). Look through the court cards until you find one that seems to reflect your inner sense of who you are. Set this card at the top of the pattern, above Kether. We call this card the Significator, since it signifies the totality of who you are at this point in your life. Though it would be presumptious to compare the Significator to the En Sof, we might say that because this single card represents the whole self it becomes in a sense beyond our comprehension.

With one card taken out we have seventy-seven cards. Since there are eleven sephiroth (including Da'ath), we can put down seven cards for each position. The interpretations become partly a matter of how the cards in any line fit together. Obviously, this method takes considerable time (I once did a full deck reading that lasted seven and a half hours), and most people will want to make sure they know the cards very well before they attempt it. Do not think, however, that the single card readings are somehow weaker or less meaningful. Powerful understandings can leap out at us from the juxtaposition of a single card with the intense images and meaning of a sephirah.

FURTHER READING

Anonymous. *Meditations on the Tarot.* Element, 1985.

Besserman, Perle. *The Shambhala Guide to Kabbalah and Jewish Mysticism.* Shambhala, 1997.

Case, Paul Foster. *The Tarot.* Builders of the Adytum, 1974.

Cook, Roger. *The Tree of Life.* Thames and Hudson, 1974.

Crowley, Aleister. *The Book of Thoth.* O.T.O., 1944.

———. *The Qabalah of Aleister Crowley.* Weiser, 1973 (retitled 777 *and Other Qabalistic Writings of Aleister Crowley*, Weiser, 1977).

DuQuette, Lon Milo. *The Chicken Qabalah of Rabbi Lamed ben Clifford.* Weiser, 2001.

Greer, Mary K. *Women of the Golden Dawn.* Park Street Press, 1995.

Halevi, Ze'ev ben Shimon. *Kabbalah.* Thames and Hudson, 1979.

———. *A Kabbalistic Universe.* Gateway, 1977.

Idel, Moshe. *Kabbalah: New Perspectives.* Yale University Press, 1988.

Kaplan, Aryeh. *The Bahir.* Jason Aronson, 1995.

———. *The Living Torah.* Maznaim, 1981.

———. *Meditation and Kabbalah.* Samuel Weiser, 1982.

———. *Sefer Yetzirah: The Book of Creation in Theory and Practice.* Samuel Weiser, 1997.

Kliegman, Isabel Radow. *Tarot and the Tree of Life.* Quest, 1997.

Kushner, Lawrence. *The Book of Letters.* Harper and Row, 1975.

———. *Honey from the Rock.* Harper and Row, 1977.

Lao Tzu. *The Tao Te Ching.* trans. Gia-Fu Feng and Jane English. Vintage, 1989.

———. *Tao Te Ching.* trans. Ursula K. Le Guin and J. P. Seaton. Shambhala, 1998.

Laura, Judith. *Goddess Spirituality for the 21st Century: From Kabbalah to Quantum Physics.* Triangle Books, 1997.

Mathers, S. L. M. *Kabbalah Unveiled: Books of the Zohar.* Routledge and Kegan Paul, 1970.

Matt, Daniel. *The Essential Kabbalah.* HarperSanFrancisco, 1995.

———. *Zohar: The Book of Enlightenment.* Paulist Press, 1983.

Meltzer, David. *Secret Garden: An Anthology in the Kabbalah.* Seabury Press, 1976.

Moore, Alan, J. H. Williams III, and Mick Gray. *Promethea.* America's Best Comics, 1999-present.

The New English Bible. Oxford University Press, Cambridge University Press, 1970.

Patai, Raphael. *The Hebrew Goddess.* Avon, 1967.

Pollack, Rachel. *The Body of the Goddess.* Element. 1997.

———. *Complete Illustrated Guide to Tarot.* Element, 1999.

———. *Der Haindl Tarot.* Knaur, 1988, Econ, 2001.

———. *Der Haindl Tarot Arbeitsbuch.* Econ, 2002.

———. "The Four Rabbis Who Entered Paradise," in *Spring 66*, Spring Journal, 1999.

———. *Seventy-Eight Degrees of Wisdom.* Thorsons, 1980, 1983, 1997.

Poncé, Charles. *Kabbalah: An Introduction and Illumination for the World Today.* Quest, 1973.

Regardie, Israel. *The Garden of Pomegranates.* Llewellyn, 1932, 1970.

Rosenberg, David. *Dreams of Being Eaten Alive: The Literary Core of Kabbalah.* Harmony House, 2000.

Rothenberg, Jerome, Harris Lenowitz, and Charles Doria, eds. *A Big Jewish Book: Poems and Other Visions of the Jews from Tribal Times to the Present.* Doubleday, 1978.

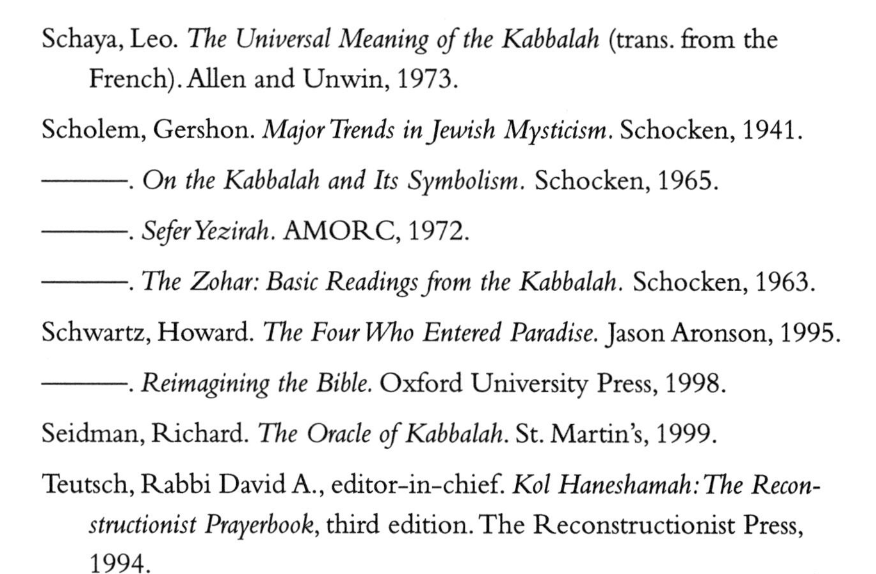

Schaya, Leo. *The Universal Meaning of the Kabbalah* (trans. from the French). Allen and Unwin, 1973.

Scholem, Gershon. *Major Trends in Jewish Mysticism*. Schocken, 1941.

———. *On the Kabbalah and Its Symbolism*. Schocken, 1965.

———. *Sefer Yezirah*. AMORC, 1972.

———. *The Zohar: Basic Readings from the Kabbalah*. Schocken, 1963.

Schwartz, Howard. *The Four Who Entered Paradise.* Jason Aronson, 1995.

———. *Reimagining the Bible.* Oxford University Press, 1998.

Seidman, Richard. *The Oracle of Kabbalah*. St. Martin's, 1999.

Teutsch, Rabbi David A., editor-in-chief. *Kol Haneshamah: The Reconstructionist Prayerbook*, third edition. The Reconstructionist Press, 1994.

Wang, Robert. *The Qabalistic Tarot*. Samuel Weiser, 1983.

Zlotowitz, Meir. *Bereishis / Genesis: A New Translation with a Commentary from Talmudic, Midrashic, and Rabbinic Sources.* Mesorah, 1977.

INDEX

TO WRITE TO THE AUTHOR

If you wish to contact the author or would like more information about this book, please write to the author in care of Llewellyn Worldwide and we will forward your request. Both the author and publisher appreciate hearing from you and learning of your enjoyment of this book and how it has helped you. Llewellyn Worldwide cannot guarantee that every letter written to the author can be answered, but all will be forwarded. Please write to:

Rachel Pollack
℅ Llewellyn Worldwide
P.O. Box 64383, Dept. 0-7387-0507-1
St. Paul, MN 55164-0383, U.S.A.

Please enclose a self-addressed stamped envelope for reply, or $1.00 to cover costs. If outside U.S.A., enclose international postal reply coupon.

Many of Llewellyn's authors have websites with additional information and resources. For more information, please visit our website:

http://www.llewellyn.com